THE Los Angeles

Times BOOK OF THE

1984 OLYM

PIC GAMES

HARRY N. ABRAMS, INC.,

PUBLISHERS, NEW YORK

Project Manager: Robert Morton
Designer: Bob McKee
Editorial Assistant: Beverly Fazio

Library of Congress Catalog Card Number: 84-70392
ISBN 0-8109-1284-8
Illustrations ©1984 *Los Angeles Times*
Published in 1984 by Harry N. Abrams, Incorporated,
New York. All rights reserved. No part of the contents
of this book may be reproduced without the written
permission of the publishers

Printed and bound in Japan

Pictures on the preceding pages:
1. U.S. shot-putter Dave Laut. Photo by Patrick Downs/*Los Angeles Times*
2. Chinese weightlifter Yao Jingyuan. Photo by Baseball Magazine-sha
3. American rower, single scull. Photo by Focus on Sports
4. Dwight Stones, U.S. high jumper. Photo by Patrick Downs/*Los Angeles Times*
5. American platform diver. Photo by Dave Gatley/*Los Angeles Times*
6. Romanian gymnast on the balance beam. Photo by Gary Friedman/*Los Angeles Times*
7. Scott Johnson, U.S.A., on the pommel horse. Photo by Gary Friedman/*Los Angeles Times*
8. Sprint cyclists on the Olympic track. Photo by Randy McBride/*Los Angeles Times*
9. Evelyn Ashford, U.S.A., and Marlies Gohr, East Germany, in the 100-meter dash. Photo by Patrick Downs/*Los Angeles Times*

CONTENTS

Dwight Stones carries the flag at a U.S.-East Germany dual meet held in the Los Angeles Coliseum in 1983.
Photo by Jayne Kamin/Los Angeles Times

FOREWORD

BY OTIS CHANDLER

I am happy and pleased that the Olympic Games are returning to Los Angeles. They will be good for Los Angeles and good for the country.

I know there are many critics of the Games who have complained about everything from the inevitability of smog alerts and traffic snarls to the possibility of terrorist attacks. But I am optimistic. I look for a terrific Olympics, the most successful ever staged.

My optimism stems partly from my confidence in Los Angeles's ability to do its job well, as it did in 1932, and partly from my passion for sports. Sports are happy events and they have always been one of the most important aspects of my life. I've been involved in games since I was a kid and I'm still playing them. Winning five gold medals in track and swimming in the Senior Olympics may not be as rewarding as winning them in the Olympic Games, but I hope that I have been able to demonstrate in my life that one can have a family, a career and also an enjoyable time in sports—even when you're a fifty-six-year-old grandfather.

Sports can make this a healthier country. Many corporations, including Times Mirror, have fitness programs which lead to better health, nutrition and exercise among their employees. Competitive sports have sharpened my business instincts.

I marvel at the skill, agility and strength of young athletes today. The competitors we will see in the Olympic Games this summer jump and throw farther, leap higher, swim and run faster and lift heavier weights than ever before.

As a young man, I dreamed of making the Olympic team, but the Games came at the wrong time in my career. In 1948, while a sophomore at Stanford University, I qualified for the Olympic Trials as a shot-putter. I finished fifth but only three made the team.

In 1950 and 1951 I was ranked second in the world but there were no Olympic Games in those years. In 1952 I was so confident I would make the team and go to Helsinki, I had my passport ready. Then I hurt my wrist and again failed to qualify.

To give you an idea of how athletes have improved, when I ranked No. 2, Parry O'Brien had not yet broken the 60-foot barrier. In the 1980 Games at Moscow, a Russian exceeded 70 feet, and the world record today is held by Udo Beyer of East Germany at 72 feet 10¾ inches.

I have many happy memories of past Olympics. I was only five years old in 1932 so I don't remember much about the first Los Angeles Games, but since then there have been many unforgettable moments: Jesse Owens winning four gold medals at Berlin in 1936; seventeen-year-old Bob Mathias winning the decathlon in 1948 at London; Parry O'Brien's back-to-back victories in the shot put in 1952 and 1956; Al Oerter's four straight gold medals in the discus; Billy Mills winning the 10,000 meters at Tokyo; Bob Beamon's astonishing 29-foot-plus long jump at Mexico City; Mark Spitz's seven gold medals in swimming at Munich; Bruce Jenner's record-breaking decathlon victory at Montreal and the U.S. hockey team's emotional triumph over the Soviet Union at Lake Placid.

I saw my first live Olympic Games at Rome in 1960 and came away impressed by the splendid performances of the great New Zealand and Australian runners Peter Snell in the 800 and Herb Elliott in the 1,500; Ethiopia's little barefooted marathoner, Abebe Bikila, and the United States sprinter Wilma Rudolph, who won both the 100 and 200. A young U.S. boxer named Cassius Clay showed a lot of promise as he won the light-heavyweight gold medal.

Every Olympics seems to produce champions who remain celebrities long after they retire from competition, stars such as Jim Thorpe, Johnny Weissmuller, Babe Didrikson, Jesse Owens and Paavo Nurmi. Who will be the superstars of 1984?

In this book, writers for the Los Angeles Times, who have become specialists in the twenty-one Olympic sports, identify some of the athletes who are expected to win gold medals and fame at Los Angeles this summer. The writers have traveled the nation and much of Europe to gather background on the stars of their sport. Their bylines have appeared from Moscow, Budapest, Berlin, Leipzig, Helsinki, Zurich, London, Rome, Prague, Kiev, Amsterdam and Havana. Never have so many sportswriters roamed so far in search of stories. Their reports also include a brief history of their sport and the rules that govern it. Most of the photographs are the work of Times cameramen, who are also becoming experts in specific Olympic sports.

It is appropriate, I believe, for the Times to publish a book on the Olympic Games. The Times and my family have been closely involved with the world's most important athletic event starting with the 1932 Games in Los Angeles. My grandfather, Harry Chandler, who was then publisher of the Times, was a member of an organization made up of civic-minded businessmen who played an important role in bringing the Olympics to Los Angeles, and my uncle, John Jewett Garland, succeeded his father, William May Garland, as a member of the International Olympic Committee in 1948.

Bill Henry, a former Times sports editor, was also active in getting the Olympics for Los Angeles and served as Sports Technical Director for the 1932 Games. Henry's expertise was also sought by IOC President Count de Baillet Latour for the 1936 Games at Berlin, which Henry covered for the Times.

As publisher of the Times, I strongly supported earlier bids by Los Angeles to obtain the Olympic Games. And as Chairman of the Board and Editor-in-Chief, I support Times Mirror's role as an official sponsor for the 1984 Games. For ten weeks this summer, the company will sponsor the Olympic Arts Festival.

The Times's commitment to the 1984 Games is immense. Olympic stories have filled hundreds of columns since the Games were awarded to the city in 1978. But they were only the start of the flood of Olympic news. Every day for three weeks this summer, a special Olympics section will be published, incorporating the expertise and creativity of virtually every department of the newspaper.

Never has the paper expended so much space and time and mustered so much manpower for an editorial project. It is our commitment to excellence. We hope it matches the performances of the great athletes who will compete in the Los Angeles arenas this summer.

OLYMPIC HISTORY

BY KENNETH REICH

"We may sing of no contest greater than Olympia," wrote Pindar, greatest of the ancient Greek choral lyricists, in the fifth century before Christ. "Just as water is the most precious of all the elements, just as gold is the most valuable of all goods, and just as the sun shines brighter than any other star, so shines Olympia, putting all other games into the shade."

Some 2,500 years later, on September 26, 1979, one of the eminent guardians of the modern Olympic Games was asked what significance she saw in the signing of what was by far the largest television contract yet for the rights to show the Games in a single country—$225 million by the ABC network for the United States in 1984. "Nothing is too fantastic for the Olympics," Monique Berlioux, the staff director of the International Olympic Committee, said proudly.

In that regard, nothing has changed. The games established so long ago, revived at the end of the nineteenth century by a French nobleman who, like the ancient Greeks, believed that rigorous competition would bring forth the best human characteristics, are still at center stage. But the Olympics of today dwarf in their complexity and their critical problems the single, simple 192-meter footrace that was held to honor the Olympian god Zeus beside the river Alpheios in the western Peloponnese and was won by a cook named Koroibos in 776 B.C. In place of a few Greek city-states, more than 150 countries and territories throughout the world are eligible to send athletes to march into the Los Angeles Coliseum at the 1984 opening ceremonies. And instead of one event, there will be 367, scattered along nearly two hundred miles of the California coast, not to mention two soccer sites in Maryland and Massachusetts.

"In ancient Greece, the spirit of competition and the sporting ideal acquired a central position in society for the first time in human history," noted publisher George A. Christopoulos, in prefacing the book *Athletics in Ancient Greece.* The origins of the Olympics are lost in myths of competing Greek gods, of Zeus wrestling Kronos or of Apollo racing Hermes. Competitions may have been held in Olympia for hundreds of years preceding 776 B.C. But that date has

been set forth as the formal beginning, and it is also the beginning of accurately dated history. "Chronology only begins to be precise enough to specify the exact year of any event after the First Olympiad," H.G. Wells said in his *Outline of History.*

From the first, the Games were held every four years at the hottest time of the summer and were marked by a truce that lasted long enough to allow both athletes and spectators to come safely from their homes. At the outset, the truce was a month long, but later, as the fame of the Olympics spread and participants came from more and more distant Greek cities, it was extended to three months. During the truce, not only did all hostilities among Greek communities cease, but free right of passage to Olympia was given and no death penalty could be carried out. Armed individuals or army units were forbidden to enter the Olympic area. Thousands of years later, the Baron Pierre de Coubertin, founder of the modern Games, was to lament that in the days of antiquity, wars stopped for the Olympics, but in the twentieth century, the Games stopped for wars.

The site of the Games was Zeus's most sacred place, a grove named Altis on a flood plain in a valley that even today retains a mystic beauty.

From his churning arms and long stride, the runner pictured on this amphora from Rhodes is racing in a sprint. Running competitions at varying distances were part of the earliest games festivals at Olympia. Photo Hirmer Verlag

The stadium that was eventually constructed for the races at Olympia was about 643 feet long and 97 feet wide. Approximately forty thousand spectators could sit on the slopes surrounding the sandy track. As the years went by, the competitions grew in number and diversity and the days of the Games were extended from one to, most commonly, five. Sacrifices of animals took place. A great Temple of Zeus, containing a forty-foot-high gold and ivory statue of the god, was built, as were athletic facilities, a gymnasium, a swimming pool, a horse race course. After the sixtieth Olympiad, scores of statues of Olympic victors came to adorn the premises. There were service facilities for the spectators, who by rule were all male. The athletes competed oiled and naked. Women were barred on penalty of being thrown over a cliff, although for a time in other years, there were separate women's games.

New events were added only gradually. In 724 B.C., a double-length foot-race was inaugurated. Four years later, a long-distance race began, about two and a half miles. In 708 B.C., the pentathlon and wrestling were added; in 688 B.C. boxing; in 680 B.C. the Tethrippon, a four-horse chariot race; in 648 B.C. the Pankration, a type of combined wrestling and boxing so rough that it was frequently fatal to one or even both combatants; in 632 B.C. a footrace and wrestling for boys; in 616 B.C. boxing for boys; in 520 B.C. a race in armor, and so on. In the ancient Games, there was no marathon.

At first, the only prizes were simple crowns cut from a sacred wild olive tree that grew near the Temple of Zeus. The second- and third-place finishers got nothing. But, as B. Kyrkos notes in his book *The Olympic Games,* from the fifth century B.C. on, "despite the fact that the prize...was simply a crown, a number of cities began to honor the victors by offering them goods or money or exemptions that could be measured in terms of money....The phenomenon of athletes competing solely for money gradually took on serious dimensions—a development that proved impossible to arrest. Professionalism in sport was not an isolated phenomenon." Some athletes even hired themselves out to compete for various cities.

Both De Coubertin and the American sportsman Avery Brundage, who for twenty years beginning in the 1950s ruled the International Olympic Committee with an iron hand, were fond, after the modern Games were revived, of talking as if the ancient Games had been models of amateurism. That was clearly not the case. In fact, David Young, professor of classics at the University of California at Santa Barbara, has calculated on the basis of historic evidence that Athens used to pay its Olympic champions the equivalent of $338,800 tax-free, the amount a skilled craftsman of that day might earn in fourteen years.

The ancient Games lasted nearly 1,200 years, but their ideals were frequently corrupted. Indeed, they outlived the faith in the traditional Greek religion and lost their religious significance. Like the modern Games, they tended to become commercialized. The Roman Emperor Nero showed up and won the chariot race in A.D. 65, after forcing his opponents to withdraw, although his victory was later invalidated. But through invasions and disruptions, through the conquest of Greece by the Romans, the Games survived, until finally, in A.D. 393, Theodosius I, the first Christian Emperor of Rome, banned their continuance as part of a campaign against rituals of pagan origin. There had been nearly three hundred Olympiads.

As the years passed, evidence that the Olympics had ever been held on their ancient site vanished. The Temple of Zeus was burned, perhaps in accord with an order by Theodosius, in A.D. 426. A flood tore away part of the Altis and the river Alpheios permanently shifted its course to run through the grounds. More than twelve feet of silt covered the place where the Games had been celebrated. And it was not until 1766 that the site was rediscovered by the Englishman Richard Chandler, a collector of antiques on an exploratory mission. Full-scale excavations did not begin until the German government, with the consent of the Greeks, undertook them in 1875.

But the legend of the Games had not died. They lived in classic writings, and as international communications improved, thoughts of a revival began to stir. There were sporadic attempts to hold Olympic Games in England in the eighteenth century. But it was not until De Coubertin that their revival was to prove lasting.

Baron de Coubertin, born in 1863, became convinced as a young man that France, defeated by the Prussians in the war of 1871, would be doing better in world affairs were it as devoted to youthful sports and physical fitness as England. Even before he was twenty-five, he had begun to organize groups to advance sports competition, and in 1889 he founded the Union of French Societies of Athletic Sports. On the occasion of its fifth anniversary, he declared, "It is necessary to internationalize sports; it is necessary to revive the Olympic Games." De Coubertin organized a conference at the Sorbonne and invited foreign as well as French dignitaries to hear his proposal. On June 23, 1894, the seventy-eight delegates from nine countries unanimously gave their assent to it and adopted a motto for the Games suggested by Father Henri-Martin Didon: "Citius, Altius, Fortius" (faster, higher, stronger). De Coubertin was authorized to form an international committee to coordinate the Games, which would be held for the first time in Athens, in 1896.

The first modern Games barely came off, and then only after several determined interventions with reluctant Greek authorities by De Coubertin. Twelve nations participated in the Athens Games and the contingent that won the most medals was a decidedly amateur thirteen-member American team. Not the best amateurs the United States could have sent, either.

As De Coubertin himself later wrote to Olympic historian Bill Henry, "It is hard for anyone to realize the very slow formation of the International Olympic Committee. It did not enter into real action until after the beginning of the century. Until then, they were friends gathering around me with

A Greek archer characteristically competed in the nude as all early Olympians did. Photo Martin V. Wagner–Museum

much indifference and pleasant smiles. As to public opinion, there was none. No help could come from there, either financial or moral. It has been said that Olympism was in the air and likely to be revived somehow or other. It was not. It was born artificially."

Yet by the 1912 Stockholm Games, just sixteen years after their revival, the Olympics had caught on as world theater and were so solidly established that their progress as an international event could be impeded only temporarily by World War I, which forced a hiatus. Stockholm was the scene of one of the first great modern Olympic athletic dramas—the victories of the American Indian athlete Jim Thorpe in the pentathlon and decathlon. When, on the victory stand after the decathlon competition, Sweden's King Gustav told Thorpe, "Sir, you are the greatest athlete in the world," Thorpe replied, "Thanks, King." Yet a year later, Thorpe, having admitted that he had played professional baseball for about two dollars a day in 1909 and 1910, had his medals stripped from him. One of the longest and most celebrated of Olympic controversies followed, and it was not until 1983 that, to the delight of Thorpe's family, the medals were restored to him posthumously at a ceremony by international Olympic authorities.

De Coubertin ruled the aristocratic, self-perpetuating IOC, whose early members were chosen personally by him, until 1925, when he retired. And as *Los Angeles Times* writer Bob Oates has observed, the modern Games, in so many of their highly popular ceremonial aspects, are his creation. "He dreamed up the distinctive Olympic flag with its five interlocked rings (symbolizing five continents) in the colors blue, yellow, black, green and red on a peaceful white field," Oates noted. "After all these decades, ticket buyers are still lining up to be seduced by Coubertin's pageantry—the fiery Olympic torch... the magnificent opening-day parade of nations, the victory celebrations and the presentation of gold, silver and bronze medals, the playing of the Olympic anthem...the touching last-day ceremonies and all the rest.... These theatrical trimmings, which have nothing to do with sports, although they're so familiar now they're taken for granted, are a reminder that Coubertin—son of an artist—spent a quarter century tailoring the Olympics to his personal tastes."

But even from their earliest days, De Coubertin's Games suffered from contradictions that were to lead to trouble.

Watched by his trainer, who holds a javelin, a Greek athlete practices his take-off stance for the long jump. In his hands are shaped stone weights, which he swings forward for momentum and then drops while in the air before landing. Photo Museum of Fine Arts, Boston

Wrestling is frequently pictured on Greek vases and was widely practiced over a long period, yet no one knows precisely what rules the ancients followed. Photo Hirmer Verlag

An early Greek wall painting depicts a diver plunging into the sea from a platform clearly built for the purpose. Diving as a skilled sport obviously had its origins long ago. Photo by Josephine Powell

The design of the IOC was internationalist. Its members were not supposed to be representatives of the countries from which they came, but representatives of the world Olympic movement in those countries. The Games themselves were supposed to be contests not between nations, but between individuals. But the structure of the Olympic movement was mainly along national lines. It was not long before national interests, national flags, national rivalries were asserting themselves, and before the individual athletes were primarily identified as Americans or English or Chinese. The acceptance of team sports such as soccer, basketball and hockey accentuated this trend. Just recently, in late 1983, the IOC executive board has again reaffirmed the principle of a Games structured nationalistically by ruling that an otherwise qualified Brazilian athlete could not compete in the Sarajevo Winter Olympics because the Brazilian Olympic Committee decided not to field a team.

De Coubertin, becoming like many of his successors more internationally minded as his years of leading the IOC lengthened, moved the headquarters of the organization to neutral Lausanne, Switzerland, during World War I to emphasize its independence and impartiality. Even Avery Brundage, who came to the IOC as an arch-conservative American businessman prone to accuse opponents of association with Communism, ended up as IOC president working hard to bring the Com-

munist countries, led by the Soviet Union, into the Games and incorporate Eastern bloc members as full working partners.

From De Coubertin through the latest IOC president, Spain's Juan Antonio Samaranch, there has always been the desire to make the Games more universal. Quadrennial Winter Games were introduced at Chamonix, France, in 1924. The Soviet Union was permitted to join the Olympic movement at the Helsinki Games in 1952. One hundred and fifty-four countries and territories are now eligible to participate in the Summer Games and, to encourage the participation of even the tiniest and poorest, the IOC has voted to pay the way of as many as four athletes and two officials from each. De Coubertin was willing to take the Olympics to relatively remote St. Louis, Missouri, thousands of miles from their European origins, when they were still struggling to get started in 1904. He felt that one of the goals of the Olympic movement should be to spread the Games into new areas, to enhance the development of amateur sport in these places both by interesting their youth and providing new sports facilities. It was an idea that still could command a majority of the IOC members at the Baden-Baden Congress in 1981, when they voted approval of both summer and winter Olympic sites for the 1988 Games that were totally new, Seoul, South Korea, and Calgary, Canada, despite, at least in Seoul's case, the political problems

attendant on such a selection.

Los Angeles, along with London and Paris, is one of only three cities serving twice as a summer Olympic host. The 1932 Los Angeles Games were not without controversy, but they produced spirited competition, many world records and such innovations as the first specially constructed Olympic Village for the athletes.

The first great political crisis—but not the last—to afflict the Games arose with the 1936 Berlin Olympics, sometimes called the "Nazi Olympics." As it turned out, the black American athlete Jesse Owens became the greatest hero of American Olympic history at these Games, personally contradicting dictator Adolf Hitler's myth of Aryan superiority by winning four gold medals. Even before Owens could compete, there was an unseemly struggle over whether America should boycott the Games in protest against Nazi Germany's failure to adhere to its promises to the IOC not to discriminate against Jewish athletes.

When one of the American IOC members, Ernest Lee Jahncke, wrote the Belgian count who was then IOC president, Henri de Baillet-Latour, protesting his failure to force the Nazi authorities to live up to their commitments, Baillet-Latour responded angrily, demanded Jahncke's resignation from the IOC and, when he refused, saw to his expulsion. Replacing him on the IOC was Brundage, who strongly supported American participation in the

One of the earliest Olympic events was the discus, though the object then was made of stone and weighed heaven knows how much. At the first modern Games in 1896, American Robert Garrett tossed the two-kilogram disk just over 95½ feet. Today's winning mark must more than double that distance.
Photo Brogi

Games. Baillet-Latour did prevail on Hitler to remove signs from the Olympic villages saying that Jews and dogs were not allowed, but he failed ultimately to protect even part-Jews who were active in the German Olympic movement.

In his 1979 book *The Politics of the Olympic Games,* Richard Espy decried the fact that as the Games have become bigger and more successful, they have "provided a spectacle of nationalism and all the world's competing interests." If this was true in Berlin in 1936, it has become even more evident since the 1964 Games in Tokyo. The Olympics have become a victim of their own great popular success, unfortunately drawing to themselves every kind of political faction that is seeking publicity and that finds the Games a stage that commands, as surely as any international event, instantaneous world attention.

So, in Mexico City in 1968, student dissidents seeking to capitalize on the Games organized mass demonstrations that were crushed brutally by the government, with the loss of scores of

lives. At the same Games, U.S. black-power advocates made their point by raising closed fists on the victory stand. In 1972, Palestinian terrorists scaled the walls of the Munich Olympic Village and the ensuing massacre cost the lives of eleven Israeli athletes in one of the most horrifying terrorist incidents of the postwar era. In 1976, twenty-eight African countries boycotted the Montreal Games. The ostensible reason was the participation in the Games of New Zealand athletes, because a New Zealand rugby team, which had nothing to do with that country's Olympic team, had competed against a segregated South African rugby team. (South African participation in Montreal was not in question; South Africa had been expelled from the Games for its apartheid policies three Olympics before.) Montreal also saw the unceremonious barring of Taiwanese athletes from the Games by the Canadian government, in violation of Olympic rules, simply because Canada diplomatically recognized China and not Taiwan.

The political problems reached a new high when the 1980 Games became the focal point of superpower contentiousness. After the December, 1979, Soviet invasion of Afghanistan, the Carter Administration in the U.S. demanded that the Games the next summer be either moved from Moscow or boycotted. When the IOC unanimously refused to either postpone or move them, then-President Jimmy Carter called for a worldwide boycott. He told American athletes, many of whom still wanted to compete in the Games, at a White House meeting that as a sacrifice to enhance the chances of world peace they would be forced to abandon their Moscow plans. The United States Olympic Committee voted its reluctant acquiescence by a two-to-one margin, and eventually sixty-four other countries, including Canada, West Germany and Japan, joined the United States in the boycott. As the IOC president at the time, Ireland's Lord Killanin, wrote later in his book of memoirs, the Moscow Games turned out to be "joyless."

But the boycott also demonstrated the resilience of the international Olympic movement. Many of the individual national Olympic committees followed the lead of those in Britain, France and Italy in defying their governments' wishes and sending athletes to Moscow. The IOC itself stuck together and its leaders maneuvered skillfully against the American government to go forward with the Games. It was an IOC idea for national committees who desired to go to Moscow, but at

the same time protest in some way against the Afghan invasion, to come to the Games under the Olympic flag rather than their national flags and have the Olympic hymn played at medal ceremonies rather than their own national anthems. Several of the committees adopted this plan.

The Olympic movement—which now has a many-layered organiza-tional structure including international and national sports federations, world-wide and regional associations of na-tional Olympic committees, the huge organizing committees of forthcoming host cities and a large number of inter-organizational commissions, in addi-tion to the IOC—seems, at this point, to be coping relatively well with some of its political problems. Just providing

Although this ancient mosaic shows that women did the long jump (at left) and threw the discus in very early Olympics, it was not until 1928 that modern women were believed strong enough to heave the discus and 1948 that they were permitted to try long jumping. Photo Fototeca Unione

Not a thinker, but a slugger, this Greek
bronze sculpture shows a boxer—his fists
wrapped in leather—waiting for the call to
do battle. Photo Hirmer Verlag

security protection for the Games has become in itself a massive undertaking, with expenditures since Munich running well over $100 million for each of the summer host cities. Fifty-five different law enforcement agencies participated in the first major security-planning exercise for the Los Angeles Games. Still, there have been no terrorist incidents at either the Summer or Winter Games since 1972.

Meanwhile, the Olympics themselves have become even greater popular successes, thanks in large part to world television. By some estimates, the audience in 1984 will be as high as 2.5 billion persons, more than half the world's population. As recently as 1960, the rights to show the Rome Games on television were sold for a worldwide total of $1 million. The American rights alone for the Los Angeles Games went for $225 million. As author Espy noted in *The Politics of the Olympic Games,* "In large measure, television has helped to make the Games the spectacle they are today by opening the Games to a mass audience...enlarging [their] concept."

Espy was not applauding the development. "Time schedules are changed for television," he wrote. "Rule changes are made in sport to increase fan interest and advertising becomes prevalent....What results is not a forum for athletic competition, but an extravaganza that reflects and enhances the competitive and divisive interests in the world."

But it is great theater, and many would disagree with Espy's view that it's not sport. Certain sports—such as ice hockey and gymnastics—have been widely popularized among those watching the Olympic Games on television. The drama of the American ice hockey team defeating the Soviet team at the 1980 Lake Placid Winter Games or the triumph of the young Romanian gymnast Nadia Comaneci at Montreal inspired many and may have gone a long way to fulfill De Coubertin's dream of the universal propagation of sport.

But De Coubertin, and certainly Brundage, would probably have been appalled to see how expensive some of the recent Games have become. The mayor of Montreal, Jean Drapeau, declared in advance that the Games he organized "can no more have a deficit than a man can have a baby." But they did, a deficit of $1 billion that the citizens of his city and Canada's Quebec province will be paying off through the end of the century. The costs included $800 million to construct the main Olympic stadium, which, while it will have long-term use,

American women have come a long way since the first female squad was formed at Kansas University in 1903. James Naismith, who invented the game in 1891, later coached at Kansas.

has never been quite satisfactorily completed. The Moscow Games are estimated to have cost the Soviets $9 billion, although there will probably never be a reliable accounting.

In part, the private financing of the more economical Los Angeles Olympic effort is a reaction to such heavy costs. Seventy-three percent of the voters of the City of Los Angeles approved an amendment to the city charter that prohibited most municipal government expenditures on the Games unless the city was guaranteed reimbursement. The Los Angeles Games are expected to have a total cost, including federally paid security, of not much over $600 million. Advance indications are that the planned 1988 Games in Seoul may revert to the pattern of higher costs, since there has already been a massive injection of government funds for construction of new athletic facilities.

One of the reasons for the high costs is the rather steady increase in the number of Olympic sports and events within those sports, including the addition of many events for women, such as the marathon in 1984. The process continues, and at the most recent World Olympic Congress in 1981 most of those addressing the question of "giganticism" at the Games took the position that it had not gone too far. Two more sports will be added at the Seoul Games, tennis and

table tennis, and there is continuing pressure to add even more sports.

Allen Guttmann, in his book on the life of Brundage, *The Games Must Go On,* quotes him asking in 1972: "Is ice dancing an athletic sport or not? The next thing we will have is an application to add synchronized swimming (which is a form of water vaudeville), fly casting for fishermen, billiards, bowling, sky diving, and baton twirling. Where does it stop?" It may be worth noting that while the Los Angeles Games will not have fly casting, billiards, bowling, sky diving or baton twirling, they will have synchronized swimming, and tickets for it were among the first to sell out. They will also have rhythmic gymnastics, which, while it may not be baton twirling, is close.

All this has contributed to the steadily growing commercialism of the Games. Brundage, in the late 1940s and early 1950s, Guttmann points out, waged a personal campaign against the practice of the Helms Bakery in Southern California using the Olympic

rings in its advertising and saying it produced the Olympic bread. But as the years passed, such scruples among Olympic leaders faded, as long as the companies in question were willing to pay for use of the Olympic symbols. Even the Moscow Olympics, had it not been boycotted, would have had many American commercial sponsors, including Coca-Cola—thereby gaining for itself an entry into the potentially immense Soviet soft-drink market—and Levi Strauss, which would have provided uniforms for the Soviet Olympic staff. Lake Placid had hundreds of commercial sponsorships, including an "official" chewing tobacco, and the Los Angeles Games, while being considerably more restrained in the number of sponsorships it is willing to sell, is nonetheless charging its sponsors the largest sums ever and has an "official" beer, Budweiser.

It has grown somewhat confusing, because companies that are not able to buy into the sponsorships of the various Olympic Games can buy

sponsorships of the various national teams, or simply television sponsorships. With the proliferation of Olympic logos, and the IOC beginning to move into fields of selling sponsorships that have hitherto been restricted to the local organizing committees or the national Olympic committees, it has become difficult to tell all the players in the Olympic commercial games without a program. Litigation has even cropped up. The United States Olympic Committee recently sued to prevent a firm the IOC had retained to market Olympic symbols from infringing on its commercial rights in America.

Meanwhile, there has been a trend, as there was in the ancient games, toward professionalism. De Coubertin and Brundage were strong apostles of amateurism, but soon after their inception the modern Games were plagued by instances of professionalism and as the pressure grew for improved performances, as world records fell and popular involvement deepened, so the need grew for

lengthier, more expensive training. With the advent of Soviet participation in the Games, it became clear that many of the Olympic competitors from the Eastern bloc were indeed professionals in the sense that they devoted themselves to sport full-time and earned their livelihood from their sports activities.

For several Olympics, highly successful American athletes such as Mark Spitz and Bruce Jenner have left amateur ranks after the Games and made substantial fortunes from endorsements of commercial products and personal appearances. Meanwhile, in recent years, driven to match Eastern bloc athletic performances, more and more Western athletes who are still in Olympic competition have been taking sizable subsidies during their training. Some have begun taking substantial sums under the table from promoters of major non-Olympic meets. Gradually, the international sports bodies have moved to legitimize existing practices. At the 1983 IOC annual meeting in New Delhi,

Opposite: *In 1948, at London, in the first Olympic Games held since Berlin 1936, American Bob Mathias won the decathlon, repeating the feat in 1952. AP Photo*

Left: *Olga Korbut changed the face of modern women's gymnastics with her elfin charm and daring, but her performances were spotty. At Munich in 1972 she placed seventh in the all-around, though she had a second in the uneven parallel bars and two firsts in balance beam and floor exercise. AP Wirephoto*

signs of an outright acceptance of some avowed professionals surfaced when it was agreed that in the demonstration sport of tennis in Los Angeles, everyone twenty years of age or under, professional or amateur, would be eligible to compete. It was tentatively agreed that professionals under twenty-three years of age could compete in preliminary soccer competitions. Nevertheless, the present IOC leadership remains reluctant to move in this direction very quickly. Or even talk about it very explicitly.

An issue somewhat related to professionalism is the drug question. As athletes have become more professional, some have also apparently been tempted to enhance their performances by taking anabolic steroids and other muscle- and endurance-building drugs in contradiction to Olympic rules. In 1978, Killanin proclaimed steroids to be one of the worst threats to the Games, and the Olympic community has been moving fitfully toward the implementation of ever more rigorous drug testing.

The Olympic Games, meanwhile, have become more than just a once-in-every-four-years event. Regional games, world cups and international meets of all kinds are now linked to the major Olympic organizations, which hold meetings quarterly in every part of the world. The IOC, whose expenses De Coubertin once paid out of his own pocket, now has a staff of more than fifty and an income in the present quadrennial in excess of $60 million. It pays all its members' expenses whenever they are on Olympic business, which is much of the time.

Meanwhile, the athletes' training in many cases goes on, not for the ten months that was traditional for the ancient Games, but the year-around and sometimes for many years in advance of a particular Games. The U.S. is one of the few major Olympic competitor countries that does not directly pay its Olympic committee's expenses, thereby subsidizing with public funds the national athletes. The practice of sports medicine to enhance athletic performance, and even biomechanics,

to develop better athletic techniques, is expanding rapidly.

And, 2,760 years after that day in Greece when the cook Koroibos won the first official Olympic footrace, Pindar's words are still appropriate: "Just as water is the most precious of all the elements, just as gold is the most valuable of all goods, and just as the sun shines brighter than any other star, so shines Olympia, putting all other games into the shade."

1932 OLYMPICS

BY RANDY HARVEY

In 1920, Los Angeles was a city on the make. It was growing in population and national prominence, but, to the rest of the world, it was better known for its close proximity to Hollywood. The City of Angels had second billing to City of Barrymores.

When civic leaders decided to improve this situation by making a bid to host the 1924 Olympic Games, the only roadblock as far as they were concerned was finding someone who could write the invitation in French, which, along with English, was one of the official languages of the International Olympic Committee. A bilingual secretary was found in the office of L. N. Brunswig, a local businessman, and Bob Weaver was dispatched to Europe in 1923 to deliver the invitation. He arrived late—by several years—discovering upon arrival that the 1924 Games already had been awarded to Paris and that the 1928 Games were tentatively committed to Amsterdam. Nonetheless, the IOC was impressed by Weaver's presentation and promised the 1932 Summer Olympics to Los Angeles, which gave the Los Angeles Olympic Organizing Committee nine years to prepare. But how do you prepare for a depression?

As 1932 began, there was concern that there might not even be a Summer Olympics that year. A *Los Angeles Times* editorial said, "Everyone concerned is hoping that Old Man D. Pression will be a thing of the past by the time next summer rolls around." That proved to be overly optimistic. When the United States Olympic Committee began its fund drive to send the United States athletes to Los Angeles, it originally set its goal at $350,000. Several months later, when only $34,479 had been collected, there was some sentiment among USOC officials to have the Games canceled or at least postponed. U.S. Olympic Committee President Avery Brundage, later to become IOC president, rejected those suggestions, and lowered the goal to $250,000, all but $48,000 of which eventually was collected. Still, the U.S. could afford to send only 340 athletes to Los Angeles, 60 fewer than it had entered at Amsterdam four years earlier.

The host country was more fortunate than some. Twenty of the fifty countries invited were forced to decline because of financial difficulties. By

the time Spain determined it could afford to send a team, it had only two athletes still in training. The Spanish chose not to enter. Norway was able to send five athletes only because a group of Norwegian immigrants living in Los Angeles paid their way. Brazil managed to send a team only by boarding it on a ship loaded with coffee, the steamer *Itaquiu*, which was bound for the ports of Los Angeles and San Francisco. But some of the athletes did not have the proper papers when they arrived. Forty of the sixty-nine Brazilians never were allowed ashore in Los Angeles. Those who did leave the ship were not particularly competitive, but they were enthusiastic. During a 7-3 water polo loss to Germany, the Brazilians were called for forty fouls, to four for the Germans. There were several misunderstandings during the match, most of them caused because of the language barrier between the Brazilians and the Hungarian referee, who was suspected by many to actually be the Hungarian coach. When the game ended, the Brazilians stormed out of the pool and chased the referee into the stands before they were restrained by the police. Looking back on the incident later, Sir Harold Bowden, chairman of the British team, dismissed it as mischief. "Boys will be boys and all that," he said.

Somewhat more serious was the civil war in the Olympic Village. With two factions claiming control of the government in Argentina, each sent a team to the Games. Housed next to

A commemorative medallion from the 1932 Los Angeles Summer Games. Photo by Los Angeles Times

each other, they broke into a brawl one night because of their political differences. Otherwise, there was harmony in the Olympic Village. That came as a surprise to many IOC officials, who had never considered placing all the athletes together in previous Games. When the Los Angeles Organizing Committee suggested the idea, the IOC scoffed that athletes from different countries, considering their cultural differences and ancient rivalries, could never coexist in peace with each other. But the Organizing Committee proceeded with the plans, carving out a "City of Many Tongues" on 331 acres of undeveloped land in Baldwin Hills. About ten minutes from the Olympic Stadium, known today as the Coliseum, 550 wood-frame portable houses—each 10 by 24 feet—were converted into a neighborhood that included five miles of flower-bordered streets. When the Games were concluded, the houses were sold and relocated. Following the Games, Lord David George Brownlow Cecil Burghley, a member of Parliament who won the 400-meter hurdles in 1928 but did not place in 1932, said, "The Olympic Village is the outstanding distinguishing mark between these and other Games. For the first time, the men of nations were able to become really acquainted."

Ironically, the 1984 Games in Los Angeles have been criticized because they are the first in recent years that will not have one Olympic Village for all the athletes. Athletes will be housed in three locations—on the campuses of UCLA, USC and Santa Barbara. Actually, not all the athletes were included in the 1932 Olympic Village. There were two thousand men there. Women athletes stayed at the centrally located Chapman Park Hotel. The price was the same for everyone—two dollars a day. Contact between the two sexes was discouraged. Neither was allowed to enter the headquarters of the other, although a South African woman hurdler, dressed in a sweat suit and wearing a hat to cover her long hair, did manage to sneak past the security guards one day. Even though she immediately drew a crowd, she was not discovered by the guards until moments later when she took off her hat.

The woman who attracted the most attention at the Games was Mildred

*Atop the peristyle of the Los Angeles
Coliseum, built for the 1932 Games, is the
torch where the Olympic flame will be
relighted for the 1984 Olympiad. Photo by
Art Rogers/Los Angeles Times*

An aerial view of the Olympic Village where male athletes were housed during the 1932 games. AP Photo

(Babe) Didrikson, who won two of the three events she entered—breaking records in the javelin and 80-meter hurdles—and losing a third over a rule controversy in the high jump. But the most famous athlete in Los Angeles did not even compete in the Games. Finland's incomparable distance runner, Paavo Nurmi, who had won nine gold medals in three previous Olympics, was banned after an all-day session of the International Amateur Athletic Federation forty-eight hours before the Games opened for padding his expense accounts in European meets several months earlier. There was little doubt that he was playing loosely with the IOC rules of professionalism. Of Nurmi, it was often said that he "has the lowest pulse rate and the highest asking price of any amateur running in this day." Sportswriter John Lardner once wrote that Nurmi "booked any town that had a track—and a bank." Oddly enough, Nurmi probably did not need the money. He had become wealthy as the General Motors distributor in Finland. He declared his innocence, and Finland's Olympic Committee contended that the evidence against him was of a "secondhanded nature."

Nurmi, who trained as a young boy by racing against trains, already was a legend in Finland. That had been assured eight years earlier in the Summer Olympics at Paris, where he won the 1,500 meters and then, an hour and a half later, returned to the track to win the 5,000. At one time or another, he held every world record from one to six miles. When news of his disqualification reached Helsinki, there were demonstrations in the street. His fans demanded that Finland bring its athletes home in protest over the decision, but the Finns remained. Nurmi remains one of Finland's greatest heroes. When he died in 1973, at age seventy-six, he was given a state funeral, normally reserved for former presidents. A statue of him stands near the Olympic Stadium in Helsinki.

Nurmi, the Flying Finn, and his teammates had been considered heavy favorites in the distance races at Los Angeles. In his regular pre-Olympic column for the *Los Angeles Times*, USC track coach Dean Cromwell wrote: "If the United States wants to score heavily, we will have to do it in the short races and hurdles, for when the distance events come around, the flag of Finland is going to be hauled to the victory mast so much that Nurmi and his buddies will probably have to write home for a gross of new banners." When the unsmiling Nurmi checked into the Village, he carried a violin in one hand and a hatbox in the other. He would not officially register until eleven hours later, however, when he was assured that his privacy would be guaranteed. But most of his Finnish teammates had more security than they wanted. The word spread before the Games began that the Finns would not be available for interviews in their Village houses and that telephone calls to them would be closely screened. The cold Finnish nature in general, and Nurmi, specifically, were blamed by much of the press for the difficulty in approaching the athletes. But it turned out to be the crafty work of one of Nurmi's enterprising teammates, who spread word of restrictions, even though officially there were none, and then charged members of the press a fee for arranging interviews. The culprit was discovered when some of the other Finns began complaining that they were not receiving as much media attention as the athletes from other countries.

But Nurmi was not one of the Finns to complain. When reporters approached him, he said, "No speak English." He certainly did not like attention and there was reason to believe he did not like people. Many years later, *Los Angeles Times* columnist Jim Murray described Nurmi as "sere as the Finnish winter, as bleak as an icicle, as gloomy as the second act of an Ibsen play." Even when Nurmi did

The S.S. Tatsuta Maru steams up to San Pedro docks bearing the contingent of Japanese athletes, coaches and trainers for the 1932 Games. Photo from Delmar Watson Los Angeles Historical Archives

Downtown Los Angeles's main thoroughfare, Broadway, stood gaily decked in flags and bunting to welcome competitors and spectators in 1932. Wide World Photo

Not taking their bone-crushing too seriously, American wrestlers pose for the press in 1932. They took three gold medals in various weight classes in the freestyle and none in Greco-Roman, a proportion that still reflects in international competitions. *Wide World Photo*

A publicity photo of the 1932 Games shows seven athletes—conveniently clad in track suits—helping to erect one of the 550 dwellings of the first Olympic village. *AP Photo*

Decked with gold are 1932 water sports winners: from left to right—Michael Galitzen, gold metal in springboard diving, silver in platform; Buster Crabbe, gold metal in 400-meter freestyle (he came in fifth in the 1,500 meter); Helene Madison, gold in the 100- and 400-meter freestyles, gold in the 4 x 100-meter freestyle relay, and Georgia Coleman, gold in springboard diving and silver in platform. Photo from Delmar Watson Los Angeles Historical Archives

speak English, his responses, perhaps calculated, were often misleading. About his injured leg, which some thought would prevent him from winning a gold medal even if allowed to compete in 1932, he told one person that it was "all right." He told another it was "better." Still another, he told it was "still bad."

But there was no mistaking Nurmi's disappointment when he was disqualified from the Olympics. He was entered in Los Angeles in the marathon, the only long-distance race he never won in the Olympics. He reportedly told one companion, "I am thirty-five years old, and I cannot run forever. But I can lower the world marks now— many of my own. And I want to do it as an amateur." That was not to be. When the Games opened on July 30 at the Olympic Stadium, Nurmi watched from the stands. While Douglas Fairbanks Jr. and Amelia Earhart visited with him in the stands, Nurmi waved to his countrymen as they marched past him. Following the ceremony, as he approached his teammates in order to

ride back to the Village with them, he was accosted by police officers, who did not realize he was part of the group. As they grabbed him by the arms and tried to remove him by force, he refused to budge. Finally, he begrudgingly showed them his credentials.

Nurmi was not the only famous athlete who felt humiliated that day. Jim Thorpe, a hero twenty years earlier at the Olympics in Stockholm, was not allowed to enter the stadium for the opening ceremonies because he did not have a ticket. He eventually was recognized by a reporter and allowed to watch from the press box. He cried when the U.S. team entered the stadium. After reading of Thorpe's difficulties in the newspaper the next morning, Vice President Charles Curtis asked film mogul Louis B. Mayer to intervene. He saw to it that Thorpe was given a season pass to the Games.

Curtis officially opened the Games while President Herbert Hoover attended to more pressing duties in Washington. (Remember Old Man D. Pression.) Republicans, fearful of losing the White House to Franklin Delano Roosevelt in the November election, tried to persuade Hoover at least to address the crowd at the opening ceremonies over the radio because they feared FDR would score a public relations coup by appearing at the Games.

The opening ceremonies, produced with a Hollywood flair, were the most festive in the history of the modern Olympics. The teams were supposed to parade into the stadium in alphabetical order, but Great Britain was allowed to enter ahead of Germany. That resulted in a mild protest.

When tickets first went on sale in Los Angeles several months before the Games, a record 3,600 were sold on the first day. But sales slowed significantly in subsequent months until a few weeks before the opening ceremonies, when teams began arriving from overseas at ports in New York and San Francisco and it became obvious the Games indeed would be held despite the Depression. A crowd of more than 100,000 attended the opening ceremonies in the Olympic Stadium, which had been expanded from seating 76,000, to 105,000 in preparation for the Games. Between 40,000 and 80,000 fans attended the track and field competition daily. Tickets for the opening ceremonies cost three dollars. The price for most events was two dollars.

The only complaint that officials from other countries had with the selection of Los Angeles as host for

Mildred "Babe" Didrikson won the javelin gold medal in Los Angeles, the first time women had been permitted to compete in the event. Photo from Delmar Watson Los Angeles Historical Archives

Gold medalist Jean Shiley took honors in the women's high jump in the classic style of the day—a scissors kick, feet first over the bar. More than 12 inches have been added to her world record since 1932. Photo from Delmar Watson Los Angeles Historical Archives

the Games was the heat in Southern California. Sigfried Edstrom, head of the International Amateur Athletic Federation, vacationed in Los Angeles one summer before the Games and found the heat oppressive. In order to counter concerns about the climate, the Organizing Committee set up thermometers at various sites around town during the first two weeks of August in 1931. They were planning to file a report to the IOC, but when temperatures hovered around 100 degrees for that period, they suppressed it. To their relief, temperatures for the Olympics the next year were almost perfect.

Besides Fairbanks, an avid sports fan who often went to the Olympic Village to visit the athletes, there were other Hollywood celebrities at the opening ceremonies, including Joe E. Brown, Will Hays, Constance Bennett, Tallulah Bankhead, Gary Cooper, the Barrymores—Ethel, Lionel and John—Bing Crosby, Cary Grant, Conrad Nagel, Reginald Denny and Buster Keaton. Fairbanks and Mary Pickford gave a party for Olympic officials at Pickfair, where they showed a preview of Fairbanks's movie *Robinson Crusoe*. Producer Mayer gave a party at his Santa Monica home and another at his MGM studio, where Olympic officials saw the Barrymores filming *Rasputin*, Walter Huston and Mitchell Lewis in a wild jungle picture and Norma Shearer and Leslie Howard in *Smilin' Through*.

It was difficult to say who was more impressed by the other's presence, Olympic officials or the Hollywood stars. Among other romantic episodes, Austria's Prince Ferdinand von und zu Lichtenstein, the head of his country's delegation, fell hard for French film star Lily Damita. Lichtenstein caused a stir in the Village one day when he appeared without his mustache. He had grown the mustache in 1929 while on a three-week journey across the Gobi Desert and on his return it grew in length and fame. The prince became smitten with Damita during the 1932 Olympics and was invited to her home. When he entered, she told him, "Why, you look perfectly ghastly with that mustache." "What was there to do?" he told an interviewer later. He retired to another room, where he shaved the mustache. Upon returning, she said, "Now, you look worse."

Crestfallen, the prince returned to the Village, where he told an interviewer, "With athletes, I am a strong man. With women, well, I am not so strong."

But, as far as most of the world was concerned, Hollywood took second billing for two weeks to the athletes. They came from all types of backgrounds. Irish hammer thrower Patrick O'Callaghan was a famous psychiatrist. German middle distance runner Otto Pelzer was a celebrated physician. Finnish miler Harry Larva was a jeweler and watchmaker. The first two gold medals of the game were won by Frenchmen, one a dance instructor and the other a croupier in a gambling casino. There were even two newspaper reporters entered in the Games.

No one, however, captured the public's imagination more than Babe Didrikson. There was another Babe, who was making headlines almost daily with his home runs for the New York Yankees, but Ruth had nothing on the boyish twenty-one-year-old from Beaumont, Texas. Didrikson, who died in 1956 of cancer at age forty-five, has been called the greatest woman athlete of all time. Following the Olympics, she devoted most of her time to golf. In her prime, she won seventeen tournaments in a row. She also once pitched to Joe DiMaggio and struck him out. Besides golf and baseball, she was adept at basketball, swimming, billiards and tennis. She even tried boxing a few times. But perhaps her greatest feat came at the AAU track and field championships of 1932, when she single-handedly won the team championship by winning four events, tying for first in another and placing in two others. Finishing second was the Illinois Athletic Club, which fielded twenty-two competitors.

Didrikson's complaint in the 1932 Olympics was that she could not enter all six of the track and field events for women. She qualified in five but was allowed to compete in only three. As far as she was concerned, they were depriving her of three world records. "I'd break 'em all if they'd let me," said Didrikson, who was 5 feet 6 and weighed 128 pounds. The only woman who was in Didrikson's class as an athlete was Stella Walsh, who won the 100 meters and placed sixth in the discus. Walsh, a Polish immigrant who had lived in Cleveland since early childhood but competed for Poland because she had not applied for U.S. citizenship, was still participating in amateur athletics in her fifties. When she was murdered in Cleveland in 1980 at age sixty-nine, an innocent bystander during a robbery attempt, it was discovered that, although she had lived her life as a woman, she had nonfunctioning male sex organs and no female sex organs.

Didrikson was a drinker, a smoker and a swearer, but it was her boasting that made her unpopular with the other

When the rowing competitions were held for the 1932 Games at Long Beach, the skyline was still prickly with oil derricks.

U.S. oarsmen took three gold medals and a silver. Photo from Delmar Watson Los Angeles Historical Archives

Wilhelmina von Bremen edges Hilda Strike of Canada to give the U.S. a gold medal in the women's 4 x 100-meter relay, establishing a 1932 world record at 46.9 seconds. In 1980, the East German team cracked off a 41.6 for a new world mark. Wide World Photo

Robert Tisdall of Ireland is first and Lord David Burghley of Britain is fourth in the 400-meter hurdles of 1932. Tisdall got the gold medal but was denied his world record because he knocked over the last hurdle. Wide World Photo

The photo finish of the 100-meter dash with Tolan and Metcalfe neck and neck at the tape proved the need for reliable recording of race results, more accurate than human perception. Photo from Delmar Watson Los Angeles Historical Archives

women on the 1932 team. "She was good," high jumper Jean Shiley recalled in 1982 at a fifty-year reunion of athletes from the first Los Angeles Games. "But if you said, 'I swallowed thirty goldfish yesterday,' she'd say, 'That's nothing. I swallowed fifty.'" Shiley said the night before the high jump competition, many of the other women on the U.S. team gathered in her room. Their message? "You've got to beat her," Shiley said.

Didrikson did not care who she beat—men or women. When she was introduced to actor and playwright Fred Craven before the Games began, she greeted him with a bone-crushing handshake and challenged him to a game of golf. "If that don't suit, we'll try boxing or wrestling," she said. "No, we won't," Craven said. "You've already broken my right hand just being introduced." "Well," she said, "then I'll play dolls with you." Didrikson, who had played in only about twelve or fourteen rounds of golf before then but already was shooting 82, finally found a few sportswriters willing to play golf with her following the Games. She teamed with Grantland Rice against Paul Gallico of the New York Daily News and Braven Dyer of the Los Angeles Times at Brentwood Country Club. Babe, who had not played for six months while training for the Olympics, borrowed a set of men's clubs and shot 43 on the front nine. She also outdrove everyone in the fivesome, and she and Rice won.

That was one of several victories for Didrikson that week. On the first day

of the Games competition, she won the javelin with a throw of 143-4. "My hand slipped," she said afterward. She said she should have thrown it 155 or 160 feet. The world record was 153-4½. Three days later, in qualifying for the 80-meter hurdles, she broke the world record of 12.2 with a time of 11.8. The next day, she again broke the record with an 11.7 but was almost beaten by Evelyn Hall of Chicago. Fifty years later, Hall was still complaining that Babe elbowed her several times during the race and that she, not Didrikson, reached the tape first. In reviewing the race a week later, American officials declared the race a dead heat and ruled that Hall should be awarded a half-gold, half-silver medal, but the IOC never complied. Following the race, Grantland Rice wrote, "It would have been no killing shock to have seen Man O'War beaten at his peak—to have seen Dempsey knocked out—to have seen Babe Ruth flattened day after day. The downfall of Bobby Jones and Gene Sarazen would have left no lasting effect. But if some feminine body had reached the tape before Babe Didrikson arrived, the greatest upset of the year would have left 60,000 spectators stunned and dazed." Didrikson said, "I just wanted to make it a good race."

On the eighth day of the Games, the final day of women's track and field competition, Didrikson finally was beaten in the high jump, even though she jumped as high as anyone else. Shiley, a pretty Temple University student who was nicknamed Lindy

because she cleared five feet the same day that Charles Lindbergh completed his trans-Atlantic flight to Paris, set a world record at 5-5 ¼. Didrikson also reached that height, but her jump was not counted because her head went over the bar before her hands and feet. The rule was changed a year later to allow what was called the "western roll." She complained that the rule had never been explained to her.

That was one of numerous controversies during the track and field competition, the most serious occurring in the 5,000-meter race won by Finland's Lauri Lehtinen. He received an unexpected challenge on the final lap from Ralph Hill of Klamath Falls, Oregon. When Hill tried to pass the Finn on the outside, Lehtinen blocked his path. When Hill switched to the inside and again tried to pass, the Finn again blocked him. Twice thrown offstride, Hill was beaten at the tape by Lehtinen. The U.S. protested the race, but IAAF officials determined several hours later that the result should stand. "It looked like Lehtinen, or whatever his name is, made the mistake of zigging when he should have zagged," humorist Will Rogers wrote the next day in the Los Angeles Times. Westbrook Pegler was less flip, calling Lehtinen's action "a scandalous offense against the sport of the Olympic oath." Following the race, the people in the stands would not quit booing until the public address announcer chided them. "Remember," he said, "these people are our guests.

We must not shout... must not be impolite."

Hill diffused the tension by gracefully accepting his silver medal, but the sportsmanship he displayed was not unusual for that day. Lord Burghley, who had won the 400-meter hurdles in 1928, planned to rest instead of attending the leg-wearying 1932 opening ceremonies since he was scheduled to defend his championship the next day. But when His Hurdling Highness learned that his closest challenger, Morgan Taylor of the United States, had been chosen as his country's flag-bearer and, therefore, would have to participate in the opening ceremonies, Burghley decided it was only fair that he also march. The next day, they were both beaten by Ireland's Bob Tisdall.

Many of the other disputes were caused simply by official incompetence. Although there were dozens of working officials on the field, all of them managed to miss the best throw of French discus thrower Jules Noel because they were too busy watching the pole vault. Noel's throw might have qualified him for a medal, but he had to settle for fourth. Incredibly, the official lap-counter for the 3,000-meter steeplechase forgot to record the first lap, and, as a result, the competitors had to run an extra one. Volmaro Iso-Hollo of Finland would have won regardless, but Joe McCluskey of the U.S. dropped from second to third in the extra lap and received a bronze instead of a silver medal.

These Games marked the first use of the photoelectric timer, which proved valuable on the second day of the Games. In the 100 meters, it appeared that Ralph Metcalfe of Marquette University had just nipped Eddie Tolan of the University of Michigan. Both were timed in 10.3, breaking the twelve-year-old world record set by Charlie Paddock. The U.S. track coach, Lawson Robertson, had bet on Tolan and dutifully paid off after seeing the finish. When the race ended, Tolan was the first to congratulate his good friend Metcalfe. But the photos later revealed that Tolan was the winner. That was one of two results overturned because of the photoelectric timer, causing Will Rogers to reflect, "I think that the judges should be notified in some way who wins the various races, so they will know it on the day it happens."

Metcalfe was victimized again in the 200 meters two days later, when he finished third behind Tolan and George Simpson of the United States. American runners were accustomed to running the 200 on a straightaway,

but the IOC ruled that the race must be run on a curve because that was the way it was done in Europe. U.S. officials, however, were inexperienced at staggering the lanes. It was revealed later that Metcalfe, running in lane two, had to run two more yards than Tolan. Tolan, the only double winner among the men in track and field, and Metcalfe were two of four blacks on the U.S. team that year. They all won medals. Metcalfe, who died in 1978 at age sixty-eight, became a Democratic congressman from Chicago who took on Mayor Richard Daley's machine and its racial policies and won.

The 1936 Olympics were perhaps the most controversial ever because of the tension in the world, but that already had begun building by 1932. Japan had invaded Manchuria and renamed it Manchukuo—the first in a series of aggressions that eventually led to the United States's involvement in World War II. But the Japanese attempt to have Manchukuo accepted as an Olympic nation was rejected by the IOC. It was the first of many international bodies that failed to recognize Manchuria's new government. But Japan's athletes earned a great deal of respect in the 1932 Olympics, particularly in men's swimming. They won every event but one, the 400-meter freestyle. That was won by Buster Crabbe, who had been reared on a pineapple plantation in Hawaii. Crabbe won the gold medal by one-tenth of a second over Jean Taris of

France and later said, "That one-tenth of a second changed my life." He was able to quit his job as an eight-dollar-a-week stock clerk at a clothing store in Los Angeles and sign a movie contract. He became the second U.S. swimming champion to fill the role of Tarzan following his competitive career. The first, Johnny Weissmuller, decided to drop out of swimming after winning five gold medals in the two Olympic Games prior to 1932. "When I found out that a man with a dime in his hand could get a cup of coffee quicker than one with five Olympic championship medals pinned to his shirt, I decided to leave the amateur class," he said after signing to become Tarzan

Crabbe, who died of a heart attack at age seventy-five in April of 1983, was better known for his B-movie roles as Flash Gordon and Buck Rogers than as Tarzan, which he played only once. But he maintained a healthy rivalry with Weissmuller. "He doesn't just qualify physically as Tarzan," Crabbe said. "He qualifies mentally."

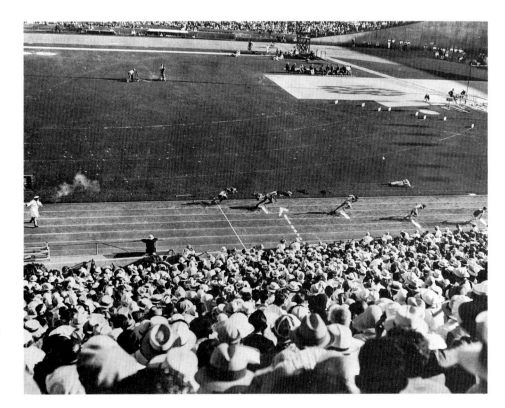

This photograph of the start of the men's 200-meter final shows clearly that Ralph Metcalfe, in lane two, was forced to run farther than the other competitors. It further shows that, contrary to one accusation, Thomas "Eddie" Tolan did not jump the gun; the puff of smoke from starter Franz Miller's pistol finds Tolan still correctly in his blocks. Photo from Delmar Watson Los Angeles Historical Archives

Another swimmer who won a gold medal and entered the movies was Eleanor Holm, who won the 100-meter backstroke. Already a member of the Ziegfeld Follies, she quit at age nineteen to train for the Olympics. But she was still a showgirl at heart. "It's great fun to swim, and a great thrill to compete in the Olympics," she said at the time. "But the moment I find my swimming making me athletic looking, giving me big bulky muscles, making me look like an Amazon rather than a woman, I'll toss it to one side." Holm no longer had to worry after 1936, when she was thrown off the U.S. team while on the way to the Munich Olympics for drinking champagne. In recent years, her claim to fame was that she was portrayed in the Barbra Streisand movie *Funny Lady.* Streisand played Fanny Brice. According to the movie version, Brice caught her husband, showman Billy Rose, in bed with Holm. Holm, later married to Rose for fourteen years, disputed the story. "Fanny Brice no more caught us in the kip than the man-in-the-moon," she said.

An interesting sidelight of the Games of 1932 was an exhibition in football, featuring West All-Stars from California, Stanford and USC against East All-Stars from Harvard, Yale and Princeton. The West won, 7-6. The athletes and spectators also were treated to a Pacific Coast League baseball game between Los Angeles and Oakland. "It may interest them [Olympic athletes] to know that in normal times in a league of this class, the salaries run from $400 to $1,000 a month, and that a major league player last season earned $85,000," a *Los Angeles Times* sportswriter wrote.

But if the Olympic athletes were interested, none of them stayed behind in Los Angeles to take advantage of the high salaries for sports stars. At least one of them, Britain's Lord Burghley, went home early so he would not miss the opening of the grouse hunting season.

Now prime real estate, this lovely, undeveloped stretch of coast between Pacific Palisades and Malibu was the site of the 100-kilometer individual road race in 1932. Italian cyclists took first, second and fourth and thus, on the basis of their cumulative times, also won the team road race medal. Photo from Delmar Watson Los Angeles Historical Archives

Right: An ancient Greek wall painting shows two young men boxing, probably competing in an early Olympic festival.

Below: The ritual spirit of historic Olympia is renewed in the opening ceremonies of each modern Games. Here is the procession of athletes at the 1972 Munich Olympics. Photo by Don Chadez/ Focus on Sports

A new Olympic-standard velodrome was built for the 1984 games at Cal State Dominquez Hills; prior to

the Games most world-class cyclists came to try out the track. Photos by Randy McBride/*Los Angeles Times*

American rider Rob Gage competing in the Grand Prix Jumping at the Griffith Park Equestrian Center in a pre-Olympic tune-up. Photo by Fitzgerald Whitney/*Los Angeles Times*

Melanie Smith, a top U.S. competitor, trains Calypso at Litchfield, Connecticut. Photo by Fitzgerald Whitney/*Los Angeles Times*

Richard McKinney of the U.S., former world champion, and other archers take aim at the 32nd World Championships

Archers from China (37C) and Luxembourg (37A) check their scores at the 1983 world championships in Long Beach, California. Photo by Steve Fontanini/*Los Angeles Times*

ARCHERY

BY ELLIOTT ALMOND

When 1976 Olympic gold medalist Darrell Pace was down to his last arrow of the four-day 1983 World Archery Championships in Long Beach, he was in good position to win his third world title.

Pace, shooting 30 meters from the target, had placed his two previous arrows inside the bull's-eye ring. As expected, his final shot also found the 10-point bull's-eye, but, to the dismay of spectators, it knocked another arrow into the 9-point range. The fluke shot cost Pace, of Hamilton, Ohio, the world championship. Rich McKinney of Glendale, Arizona, who was a point behind before Pace's final shot, finished in a first-place tie because of the mishap, and was crowned the champion on the number of 10s made over 288 shots.

Pace's final shot illustrates the intricacies of archery, a sport that leaves little room for error. Archers such as Americans Pace and McKinney, leading candidates to win a gold medal at the 1984 Olympics, rarely are off target.

In the past decade, the two have become the world's premier archers because of such precision shooting. With the United States boycotting the 1980 Olympics, Finland's Tom Poikolainen won the gold medal; Poikolainen was ninth at the world championships.

While Pace and McKinney have combined to make the U.S. an international target shooting power, they have developed quite a rivalry. Though publicly downplaying it, Pace and McKinney worry more about each other than any other contender.

The women's competition also is highlighted by two rivals, Jin Ho Kim from South Korea and Natalia Butuzova of the Soviet Union. Kim, the 1979 world champion, won the 1983 world championship by a whopping 69 points. Butuzova, and the rest of the respected Soviet archery team, did not compete because of their country's boycott of the world championship over the international incident created when a Korean airliner was shot down over Soviet territory. Kim had only her teammate, Jea Bong Jung, to compete against, and she said she would have preferred to shoot against her strongest competition to prepare for the 1984 Games.

Archers at the world championships, held at the 1984 Olympic venue in Long Beach, were as impressive as at any time in modern history. Four men— McKinney, Pace, Belgium's Marnix Vervinck and Japan's Takayoshi Matsushita—surpassed 1,300 points for one round, a rarity in archery.

When target archery was introduced to the Olympic Games in 1900 in Paris, events were conducted without internationally recognized rules, and such high scores were thought impossible. The French tried to accommodate each country by using different rules for different events. Archers again competed for medals in the 1904 and 1908 Olympics, but the sport was not included again until the 1920 Olympics in Belgium, where a special form of shooting called "Popinjay" was used. The targets in "Popinjay" are brightly colored birds made of feathers tied to the top of a mast. After that, the sport did not reappear in the games for another fifty-two years, when modern archery was reintroduced in Munich.

The sport's major breakthrough occurred in 1932, when Poland hosted the first legitimate international archery championship. At the tournament, the Fédération Internationale de Tir à l'Arc (International Archery Federation) was organized, and since then the FITA has overseen major events. Most national governing bodies recognize FITA rules, which facilitates the administering of world titles.

In a single FITA round, archers shoot six sets of arrows from distances of 90, 70, 50 and 30 meters for men, 70, 60, 50 and 30 meters for women. After each set of six arrows, called an end, arrows are retrieved and scores are recorded. At Olympic and world championship events, a double FITA round is shot. Archers must shoot seventy-two times at each set distance—a grueling exercise in concentration.

Points range from 1 to 10, and are based on which concentric color bands of the target are hit, the fewest points coming from shots on the edge, the most from the point closest to the center, the bull's-eye.

One of archery's most spectacular shots is the "Robin Hood," when an archer splits an arrow already in the target. A "Robin Hood" is considered by archers to be as rare as a hole in one in golf or a triple play in baseball.

Such precise shooting comes from continuous hours of practice and can be accomplished only with the advanced instruments modern archers use. Arrows made of aluminum tubing and with plastic vanes are aerodynamically designed to cut wind resistance and ensure more accurate shooting. Pace said he spends a week prior to a tournament tuning his bow. (A bow can cost as much as $1,500.)

Jin Ho Kim, 21, of South Korea takes aim during the World Archery Championships. She and Natalia Butuzova of the USSR are the world's best. Kim won the 1983 title. Photo by Steve Fontanini/Los Angeles Times

Above: *Rebecca Wallace* (left),
conferring with coach Sheri Rhodes at the
world championships, is considered a
bright archery prospect. At 20, she was
the youngest U.S. entrant.
Opposite: *Darrell Pace, 1976 Olympic*
gold medalist, is back for another try. Here
he zeroes in on the target at the 1983
World Archery Championships, where he
finished second to Richard McKinney,
losing on a tiebreaker. Photos by Steve
Fontanini/Los Angeles Times

CYCLING

BY SHAV GLICK

Cycling has been part of the Olympics since the Games' modern revival in 1896, and it may be the weakest sport for United States competitors in the entire Olympic program. U.S. cyclists have not won a medal of any kind since 1912, and have never won a gold medal.

This year, the U.S. has its best opportunity: women have been included in cycling for the first time. There is only one event for them, an individual road race of approximately 43 miles, but world champions Rebecca Twigg of Seattle and Connie Carpenter of Boulder, Colorado, may be as strong a one-two entry as any country will have.

Women, who have competed in the world championships since 1952, have lobbied for many years for admission to the Olympics. One event is a start, but lobbying has already begun for more events for the women in the 1988 Games in South Korea.

There are seven men's competitions; five of them (1,000-meter match sprint, 1,000-meter time trial, 4,000-meter individual pursuit, 4,000-meter team pursuit and a new event called individual points race) are on the 333.33-meter Olympic Veldrome track at California State Dominguez, and two of them (190-kilometer individual road race and 100-kilometer team time trial) on the road. Both the men's and women's road race will be held the same day at Mission Viejo in Orange County. The team time trial is on a 25-kilometer segment of the Artesia Freeway. Pursuit races involve vying for position and attempting to pass. If no passing takes place, the fastest time wins. Time trial racing features four-man teams, alternating pacing and slip-streaming.

Buoyed by their performances in the 1983 world championships in Zurich and the Pan American Games in Venezuela, U.S. riders may be a factor in several events for the first time in more than seven years. The world championship medal harvest included three gold, two silver and one bronze, although only the silver medal won by Twigg in the women's road race was for an Olympic event. Greg LeMond's stunning win in the professional road race—first ever for an American—gave hope to many amateur riders that they, too, can beat the Europeans at their own game.

In the Pan Am Games, the U.S. won six of seven gold medals, sweeping the track and losing only the men's road race. The competition was not nearly as tough as the Olympics will be, but the

improvement of American riders startled South and Central American rivals. In the Pan Am Games of 1979 in Puerto Rico, the U.S. won only one medal.

The strongest men's event may be the match sprint, an intriguing contest of wits—as well as speed—in which a pair of riders jockey for position at snail-like speeds for a couple of laps before exploding down the face of the Olympic Velodrome's 33-degree banked track in a mad dash for the finish line. Races are often won by inches, with the winner more likely coming from behind than winning from the front.

Mark Gorski, twenty-three, of La Jolla, California, won his third national championship in the last four years and finished fifth in the world championships. Nelson Vails, twenty-two, from New York City, won the Pan Am Games, which conflicted in scheduling with the world finals.

Vails is one of the few black riders in national competition and is the only U.S. rider to win as much as a heat from Gorski in the last two years. In the national finals last summer at the Olympic Velodrome, Vails forced Gorski to a third heat in a best-of-three final and it took a photo to decide the champion—Gorski by about an inch. Vails, known as "Cheetah" among cyclists, is 5-foot-9 and weighs 185 pounds, much of it in his twenty-five-inch thighs.

Because of the tactical nature of the match sprint, only the final 200 meters are timed. Vails set an American and Pan Am record of 10.6 seconds in beating former U.S. champion Les Barczewski in the finals. Only one rider is permitted from each country in the match sprint, so Gorski and Vails will have to race for the spot in the final trials in June.

Before East European bloc countries joined the Olympic movement, cycling was dominated by Italy (fourteen gold medals) and France (ten golds), but in recent years the dominant countries have been the Soviet Union and East Germany. So it is not surprising that the match sprint favorites are defending Olympic champion Lutz Hesslich of East Germany and two-time world champion Sergei Kopylov of the USSR. Gorski defeated Kopylov twice in 1983, once in Paris and again at Cal State Dominquez, but when they met in the world quarterfinals, he was outmatched. Hesslich, named the outstanding performer in an international meet last July in the Olympic Velodrome, defeated Kopylov in the world finals.

Other top U.S. hopefuls include Leonard Nitz of Flushing, New York, and Davy Grylls of San Diego, in individual pursuit, and Mark Whithead of Whittier

and Rory O'Reilly of Palo Alto, California, in the kilometer time trial.

On the road, it will be pretty much up to the women to uphold U.S. honor. Twigg, nineteen, the 1982 world pursuit champion, finished second to Sweden's Mariana Berglund in the 11-mile world road race finals at Zurich. Carpenter, twenty-six, a member of the 1972 Olympic speed skating team at age fourteen and a former sculler on the University of California's national champion women's rowing team, won the 1983 world pursuit title and two national road racing championships.

In world competition, U.S. males have not had a rider in the top ten since 1977. The best this year was Alexi Grewel's fourteenth place, while East Germany's Uwe Raab won and three teammates finished in the top ten. It wasn't much better in Caracas, where national champion Ron Kiefel was fourth and Thurlow Rogers eighth in the Pan Am Games, behind Mexico's Luis Ramos. "To say we are going to win a lot of events would be unrealistic," said Carl Leusenkamp, U.S. Olympic coach, "but we do have a lot of riders who are capable of winning a medal."

In a pre-Olympic meet on the official track, Lutz Haueissen of East Germany won the 4,000-meter pursuit final in 4:54.92. Photo by Penni Gladstone/Los Angeles Times

Opposite top: *Mark Gorski (left) finds himself in a familiar position—leading. He's the American champion in the 1,000-meter match sprint. Photo by Bob Chamberlin/Los Angeles Times*

Opposite bottom: *Yuri Lupolenko is a determined young candidate for the Soviet Union's cycling team. Photo by Penni Gladstone/Los Angeles Times*

Above: *New $3-million velodrome—with lights for night racing—was built at Cal State Dominguez Hills for the Olympics. Photo by Bob Chamberlin/Los Angeles Times*

EQUESTRIAN EVENTS

BY LYNN SIMROSS

Unlike other Olympic sports, equestrian competition requires the complete fitness and training, harmony and skill of two interdependent athletes—horse and rider. No matter how great the rider is, if the horse isn't top-notch, one that has been trained long years toward Olympic level in dressage, stadium jumping or three-day endurance, there is little likelihood of gold medals.

Equestrian competitors scour the world for just such an animal, and the price tag on mounts of Olympic caliber has risen dramatically. Before the 1984 Olympics, record prices, exceeding $500,000 for a jumper, were paid in several countries.

Because of these soaring prices, especially for Grand Prix jumping horses, U.S. owners began two years ago to set up syndicates, like those in the thoroughbred and standardbred racing communities. Now many U.S. riders in contention for a berth on this year's Olympic jumping team compete with horses belonging to private sponsors or syndicates.

Horses also are donated to the United States Equestrian Team (USET), the governing organization for American equestrians. Some horses have also been loaned to the team through the 1984 Olympics, and even for the 1988 Games in Seoul, South Korea. Right now, there are three- and four-year-old horses in training for the 1988 Games at the dressage and jumping headquarters of the USET in Gladstone, New Jersey, and at the team's three-day endurance event farm in South Hamilton, Massachusetts. "We've come a long way in the past couple of years with sponsorship and syndication," says Chrystine Jones, former USET team member who now directs show jumping for the team at Gladstone. "But a rider should have more than one horse. If you have an injury to the horse, and you have only one, obviously you're out of luck."

Each equestrian contender tries to have at least two horses able to make the team. Unfortunately, horses are delicate creatures that can develop ailments and/or lameness or suffer injuries at any time. This in itself complicates matters for Olympic contenders and countries that must choose their teams. To assure that both horse and rider are in top form as close as possible to the start of the Olympics, countries entering the equestrian competition nominate

their teams later than for any other Olympic sport.

The U.S. equestrian team will not be picked until three weeks before the Olympics begin on July 28. American team selection trials will be held in four different locations for both show jumping and three-day eventing and in three locations for dressage. European and South American equestrian entrants, because of lengthy quarantine requirements for the horse, must be chosen earlier than their American and Canadian counterparts. Horses of any breed or either sex that are a minimum of six years old may compete in the Olympics. USET representatives say that American teams have had the most success with thoroughbred geldings (castrated males).

Los Angeles Olympic dressage and stadium jumping events, and two of the three-day competitions, will be held at Santa Anita Park in Arcadia. The cross-country endurance phase of the three-day event will be held at Fairbanks Country Club near San Diego, 117 miles from Los Angeles. Because of the long travel to Fairbanks, the three-day event will include an extra rest day for the first time in Olympic history. This concession was made, and approved by the sport's world governing body, the Fédération Equestre Internationale (FEI), because of the distance the horses, not the riders, have to be transported.

Each nation may enter a maximum of fourteen riders in the Olympics, and a maximum of twenty-two horses. An individual contender or a team member can ride only one horse in each event. The other horses brought along are backups in case of injury before the event starts. Once a rider starts with a horse, the animal may not be replaced. The events, in order of the 1984 Olympic schedule, are three-day event, individual and team; team show jumping; dressage, team and individual; and individual show jumping on the final day of Olympic competition.

Although the first recorded Olympic equestrian event was the four-horse chariot race in the Games of 680 B.C., the modern Olympics did not offer equestrian competition until 1912 in Stockholm. Most equestrian teams were made up of representatives of each country's military cavalry. Prior to 1949, the U.S. Army cavalry provided riders for the American Olympic team. But in 1950, a group of sportsmen organized the nonprofit U.S. Equestrian Team, which has been responsible ever since for picking riders to represent the U.S. internationally, including the Olympics.

Since 1952 at Helsinki, women have been permitted to compete on Olympic equestrian teams. The first American

woman to become a team member that year was Marjorie B. Haynes. Lis Hartel of Denmark became the first woman to win an equestrian medal, a silver in dressage, that year.

Spectators at the L.A. Games will see the finest equestrians the world has to offer. European countries, particularly Germany and Switzerland, should be favored in show jumping, but the U.S. expects to turn out a fine, competitive team. There are at least seven top contenders for the American jumping team, three of them women. The U.S. should also field a prime three-day eventing team, again with strong opponents from several European nations. But in dressage, according to an FEI official, the U.S. is "light-years" behind the Europeans. The current world champion dressage rider is Switzerland's Christine Stuckelberger, an Olympic gold medal winner in 1976.

Dressage, the ballet of the horse world because competitors must perform a series of prescribed movements similar to those of school figures in figure skating, entails the most intense and tedious training of all equestrian competitions. Four riders and six horses may be entered by each country in dressage, though only three riders and three horses may start. In both individual and team dressage, competitors are judged on a scale of 0 to 10, with the highest total winning. Dressage requires the horse to execute a series of specific exercises in different gaits—walk, trot and canter—during a certain time limit in response to barely perceptible movements of the rider's hands, legs and weight. Dressage, it is said, originated with knights who covered themselves and their horses with protective coats of mail, holding lances in one of their hands, shields in the other. The knight, with no hand left to manage his mount, trained the horse to respond to pressure commands from his legs and shifting weight, done so subtly that his adversary would not know what his next move would be.

The showiest of equestrian competitions, perhaps, is stadium jumping (also called Grand Prix or show jumping). Horse and rider compete in an arena, over a course from 765½ to 983½ yards long, with twelve to fifteen obstacles, including five-to-six-foot fences, double or triple jumps, stone walls and a water jump. Each contestant must cover the course twice and is judged on a penalty system (points are lost if rails or fences are knocked down or the horse's foot hits the water) and on the time taken to complete the courses. The time factor is 400 meters per minute. Competitors exceeding that lose points.

Every country can enter five riders

and eight horses in the jumping and three-day events. In individual jumping, three riders and three horses may start for each nation.

In three-day eventing, four riders and four horses may start for each country; the best three will be officially placed. Long popular among Europeans, the sport of three-day eventing is taking a firm hold in the U.S. and should attract large crowds at the 1984 Games. The three-day event is a grueling test for horse and rider. It is similar to a human athlete's test of strength, endurance and physical skills in the decathlon. The same horse and rider must compete in dressage the first day, speed and endurance the second and stadium jumping the third.

The speed and endurance phase, exciting for spectators, is designed to measure the speed, boldness and jumping ability of the horse, plus the knowledge and courage of the rider. There are four sections of this phase: roads and tracks, steeplechase, another roads and tracks and, finally, cross-country. Riders, sans horses, may walk the course before the event. Horse and rider competing in the speed and endurance phase travel about fourteen miles, the last four to five of which are cross-country over twenty-seven to thirty obstacles that include fences, logs, banks and water—all ridden at a speed of about 21 miles per hour. Event officials and veterinarians examine the competing horses several times during this phase to make sure they are capable of continuing competition.

Above: *Stadium jumping is the flashiest of the equestrian events—and the most popular. Penalties are assessed for displacing crossbars. There are 12 to 15 obstacles.*

Left: *Bert Demenethy, the coach responsible for the current top-flight status of America's show-jumping team, works out at the U.S. Equestrian Team center in Gladstone, New Jersey. Demenethy will design the jumping course for the Olympics. Photos by Fitzgerald Whitney/Los Angeles Times*

MODERN PENTATHLON

BY SAM MCMANIS

The first thing a person should know about the modern pentathlon, an Olympic competition as obscure as it is diverse, is that there's nothing modern about it. To avoid confusion and perhaps do the sport a favor, the International Olympic Committee should change the name to the military pentathlon or, better yet, the historical pentathlon.

In ancient Greece, the Spartans devised a five-event competition for warriors. It consisted of a broad jump, javelin throw, 200-yard sprint, discus throw and wrestling (wrestling to death, according to some accounts).

For the 1912 Olympics in Stockholm, a new version was introduced by Baron Pierre de Coubertin, founder of the modern Olympics. The Baron designed the event around the athletic abilities that a military courier—or aide-de-camp—might require to deliver important battlefield messages. Naturally, he called it the modern pentathlon.

A courier, even as late as 1912, had to be proficient at riding an unfamiliar horse over rough terrain and across numerous obstacles, able to run cross-country when the horse would tire, swim through treacherous waters, engage in hand-to-hand combat with a sword and shoot at a moving target with a pistol. The Baron used these guidelines to come up with five events to be contested over a five-day period: a 4,000-meter run, 300-meter freestyle swim, epee fencing, 600-meter steeplechase on an unfamiliar horse and shooting with a .22 caliber pistol.

Today the events are completed in four days. The first day is for riding. Competitors guide a horse chosen in a draw over a 600-meter course that includes fifteen jumps. The object is to complete the course as quickly as possible without falls, knockdowns or refusals (the horse refusing to jump). A maximum of 1,100 points is given when a "clean" ride is completed in under 1 minute 43 seconds.

On day two, the athletes switch to epee fencing and take part in what amounts to a twelve-hour elimination tournament with each competitor facing every other in a series of three-minute, one-touch duels. Scoring is determined by the percentage of victories.

The third day is devoted to swimming. Athletes compete against the clock. A time of 3 minutes 54 seconds in the 300-meter freestyle earns 1,000 points; points are added or subtracted for each half-second faster or slower.

There are two events on the final day—shooting in the morning and the 4,000-meter (2½ mile) cross-country run in the evening. In shooting, the competitor must begin with his arm at his side and has only three seconds to raise his arm and fire at a revolving target. Each shooter has four rounds of five shots each, and the highest possible total is 200. At the beginning of the run, the points of the first four events are totaled to determine starting positions. The first-place competitor after four events earns a head start equal to his lead over the second place athlete.

In the U.S., compared to other Olympic sports, the modern pentathlon attracts few hopefuls. There are thirty senior men currently training at Fort Sam Houston in San Antonio, the only such U.S. facility. Also in training there are sixteen juniors who hope someday to become Olympians. And although there is yet no Olympic modern pentathlon competition for women, twenty-two women train for national and international meets.

With such a limited supply of athletes—albeit talented and dedicated ones—and an even sparser following from the public, it is somewhat surprising that the modern pentathlon survives in this country. But it does, thanks mostly to a commitment by the army to field the best team possible. In the Olympics, the modern pentathlon has been closely related to the military. In the 1912 Stockholm Olympics, a young and ambitious U.S. Army lieutenant named George Patton became the first American to compete in the new Olympic event. After four events, Patton had a narrow lead over the rest of the field. In the final day of competition, all he had to do to secure the gold medal was hold his own in pistol shooting. But young Patton, who prided himself as an expert marksman, placed twenty-first in shooting, dropping him to fifth in the final standings.

This year's U.S. team appears to be one of the strongest in the world, and two athletes—Bob Nieman and Mike Burley—are capable of placing in the top three in the Olympics. However, in last July's national championships in San Antonio, Dean Glenesk upset both Nieman and Burley. Nieman, in fact, didn't even make the national team, which competed in the world championships last August in Warrendorf, West Germany. Actually, it didn't matter who represented the U.S. in the world championships. The Soviet Union won the team title with a combined score of 16,014, 27 points ahead of Hungary. Individually, the Soviet Union's Anatoly

Starostin, with a tremendous performance in the last-day run, was the winner with 5,506 points. Starostin was the gold medal winner in the 1980 Olympics in Moscow and is favored to take the gold in Los Angeles.

The U.S. team feels it has a good chance at least to earn a medal. In fact, this might be the strongest the U.S. has ever been in the event. In the past the U.S. has won only three team medals (one third- and two second-place finishers) and only two Americans have won individual medals. Charles Leonard won the silver medal in 1936 in Berlin and earned the distinction of being the only man to achieve a perfect score in the shooting event. G. B. Moore won the silver at the 1948 Olympics in London.

It's rare to find an athlete who began his career as a modern pentathlete. Most pentathletes enter it after they've gone as far as they can in other sports. The Modern Pentathlon Association, based in San Antonio, places advertisements in *Runner's World* and *Swimmer's World* magazines to lure prospective pentathletes. Mike Burley was a champion prep miler in Ohio. Blair Driggs competed in gymnastics and swimming in high school. Dean Glenesk tried several different sports before attempting the modern pentathlon in 1977. And Bob Nieman turned to the modern pentathlon in desperation after failing to make the U.S. Olympic swimming team in the 1972 trials. Nieman was a successful swimmer at the Air Force Academy, but not quite world class. After the 1972 Olympic trials, Nieman faced the end of his competitive career.

"The head of the athletic department at Air Force, Wayne Baughman, called me after that and asked if I'd be interested in the modern pentathlon," Nieman said. "My reaction was natural. What's the modern pentathlon? I had no previous knowledge of it or experience in any sport other than swimming. But they convinced me to go down to Fort Sam Houston for a sixty-day trial. I broke the world record for swimming (in the modern pentathlon) my second day there, so they decided to train me full-time in all the other sports."

At thirty-six, Nieman has competed in the event for more than a decade, but trains only six hours a day because he works part-time at an architectural firm in San Antonio. Blair Driggs, who is an attorney, has a similar situation. Mike Burley, on the other hand, is a full-time lieutenant in the National Guard and has been assigned to train for the modern pentathlon. Nieman has been around the world participating in the modern pentathlon, and has seen how popular it is in countries such as Hungary, which attracted 12,000 fans for last year's world championships. But Nieman, a realist, doesn't expect the sport to grow to such proportions in the United States. At the very least, he hopes the American sporting public will be able to name the five events in the modern pentathlon by the time the 1984 Games take place. "This sport could become popular here if we do well in Los Angeles," he said. "But I guess it all depends on what ABC decides to show on TV. We might just quietly win the gold medal and go back to San Antonio."

The decathlon gets all the attention during an Olympics, but the modern pentathlon calls for greater diversity of talent. Where the decathlon is ten events in one sport, the modern pentathlon is five sports—riding, fencing, swimming, pistol shooting and running. Photos by Ken Lubas/Los Angeles Times

American John Scott takes a hurdle on Tumbleweed.

Italy's Roberto Bombrezzi scores a touch on Poland in the fencing competition.

Modern pentathlon photos by Ken Lubas/
Los Angeles Times

Mark Pohl of the U.S.A. exults after
winning the freestyle swim.

Poland's Piotr Maciaszczyk completes
the cross country run.

Ears protected, lefthander Mark Pohl
squeezes off a shot; he finished fourth
with 195 out of a possible 200.

SHOOTING

BY GORDON EDES

Leon de Lunden of Belgium holds the dubious distinction of being the only man to win a gold medal in the live-pigeon shooting competition, killing twenty-one birds in the 1900 Olympic Games in Paris. The event was subsequently abolished. The only pigeons shot at in the 1984 competition, to be held at the Prado Recreation Area, will be of the clay variety.

More than 1,100 shooters representing eighty countries are expected in Los Angeles, a field of unprecedented size competing in pistol, rifle, shotgun and air rifle events. And, for the first time, there will be a women's division, although women have competed previously right with the men—and excelled. For example, in 1976 in Montreal, Margaret Murdock, a thirty-three-year-old nurse from Topeka, Kansas, won a silver medal in the small-bore rifle competition. And a leading contender for a spot on the 1984 U.S. team is Deena Wigger, a high school senior from Columbus, Georgia, whose father, Lones Wigger, Jr., is a two-time Olympic gold medal winner and has set twenty-seven world records. Deena won the women's standard rifle three-position championship at the National Sports Festival; the event will be part of the women's competition in the 1984 Games.

Lones Wigger Jr., a lieutenant colonel in the U.S. Army, is one of the most renowned rifle competitors of all time in a sport dominated by Europeans. Wigger has competed in four previous Olympics; when he won a gold medal in Tokyo in 1964 in the small-bore rifle, three positions, he was shooting before a large crowd for the first time. His other gold came in 1972, in the 300-meter free rifle event, since discontinued.

No team prizes are awarded in shooting. Nations may enter two competitors per event. Shooters work from platformed stations that are screened off individually, except in skeet, where the shooter moves to eight different stations. The ranges are set with the sun at the shooter's back, with wind flags placed at 10-meter intervals to aid competitors in judging the wind's effect. An elapsed-time clock is used in those events that are timed. In shooting, a premium is placed on hand-eye coordination, muscle control and, of course, unshakable nerves. The margin of error is minute in a sport in which ties are often broken by awarding victory to the shooter who records the most bull's-eyes in a row.

A description of the events follows:

Small-bore, three positions: Male competitors take 120 shots at a target 50 meters away, the shots divided equally for three positions—prone, kneeling and standing. The gun is a .22 caliber long rifle weighing between 14 and 15 pounds. The target was scaled down in 1958 to a bull's-eye of less than a half-inch, smaller than a dime. No telescopic devices are used.

Small-bore, prone: For men. This is an event where the competitor does his shooting lying on his stomach. The shooter is given two hours to take 60 shots, in strings of 10. His wrist must be at least six inches off the ground. The 1980 gold medal winner in this competition, Karoly Varga of Hungary, broke his shooting hand playing soccer two days before the event, but won despite being heavily bandaged.

Moving, or running game, target: For men. The only event in which telescopic sights are allowed. Thirty shots are taken at a slow-moving target, another 30 at a fast-moving target. Both targets are 50 meters away. The target, a life-size reproduction of a boar, moves on rails and covers 10 meters in 2.5 seconds at its fastest speed, 5 seconds at its slowest. The weapon used is a .22 caliber rifle.

Air rifle: This is a new event, with competition for both men and women. An 11-pound gun is used, with women tak-ing 40 shots and men 60 at a target 10 meters away.

Free pistol: For men. Aiming at a small target (bull's-eve is less than two inches in diameter), a shooter has two and a half hours to take 60 shots. The gun's bore must be .22. Aleksandr Menlentev of the Soviet Union set a world record in the 1980 Olympics with a score of 581.

Rapid-fire pistol: For men. The shooter, using a .22 caliber pistol, has 8 seconds to fire at each of five targets 25 meters away. In the next series he has 6 seconds, the third, 4 seconds. The set of 15 shots is repeated four times.

Small-bore pistol: Women will compete, taking 30 shots on the free pistol target and 30 on the rapid-fire. The range is 25 meters.

Trap and skeet shooting: For men and women. Clay pigeons, saucers 4⅓ inches in diameter, are used. The primary difference is that in trap shooting, the pigeon is released into the air upon the competitor's signal. In skeet shooting, the competitor has no idea when the targets will be released. In trap shooting, the pigeons are sent out from ground level, at a speed of 125 miles an hour. In skeet shooting, the shooters move about to eight stations and the pigeons are released without warning from two towers, one high and one low, at a speed of 90 miles an hour.

U.S. marksman Eric Buljong pinged three gold medals—all there were to win in his events—at Pan Am and repeated the feat at the U.S. NRA matches. AP Laserphoto

Above: *Only 18 years old, Deena Wigger of Fort Benning, Georgia, won two major shooting championships in 1983. Not surprisingly, she is the daughter of Lones Wigger, Jr., winner of a silver and a gold medal at the 1964 Olympics and a gold in 1972. AP Laserphoto*

Left: *Three Canadian specialists in air rifle—a new event for 1984—take aim at a 10-meter-distant target. Narrowly beaten by the U.S. team at the Caracas Pan Am Games, they won silver medals. AP Laserphoto*

FENCING

BY JOHN DART

Fencing is a modern sport in every respect. It requires physical stamina, strength, excellent eye-hand coordination, deft and deceptive body moves and chess-like strategy. Fencers certainly *act* like other competitive athletes, often exulting after a hard-won point or bemoaning a judge's close call. For those who get close enough, fencers may even *smell* like other athletes, perspiring profusely under snugly fitting masks and heavy protective clothing.

Yet, for all the athletic characteristics of fencing, a part of the Olympic program since the Games' revival in 1896, the sport retains roots of European combat and duels centuries ago. Admittedly, the plain white garb of fencers is a far cry from movie images of colorful musketeers or finely tailored gentlemen defending their honor.

Consider the three weapons of fencing and their target areas:

■ Foil. Only touches with the sword tip on the opponent's torso are scored as points, reflecting the "duel to the death" in bygone periods when a predecessor of the foil, a heavy rapier, was employed for a piercing thrust to the vital organs. Today's 35-inch-long foil, *fleuret* in French, derives from the practice weapon for such dueling.

■ Saber. The target area is limited to the upper body, including arms and head, corresponding to the slashing tactic of cavalry soldiers who wanted to injure the rider but spare the valuable horse. The saber fencer may score points using the tip of the weapon, but, in fact, most touches are made with the edge of the blade.

■ Epee (pronounced ep-PAY). Any part of the opponent's body is a legitimate target, as long as only the point of the epee is used. The epee, despite its evolution from the dueling rapier, now reflects the "duels of honor," when once an adversary drew "first blood" from any part of his opponent, the matter of honor over a minor crime or offense was settled. Epee scoring also retains the importance of striking without being hit in the process: simultaneous touches, or touches within a fraction of a second, are scored as touches against both fencers.

Europeans, as might be expected, have been the traditional standouts in the sport of fencing. In the first half of this century, foil and epee were dominated by the Italians and French, while Hungarians led in the saber. Soviet, Hungarian and other Eastern European athletes began to excel in all three categories starting in the 1950s.

However, at the 1983 world championships, Italy and West Germany were the biggest medal winners. Also, the Cuban men's foil team won a bronze medal, and Luan Jujie of China, the women's foil runner-up in 1981, maintained her reputation as a contender by placing third last year.

Dorina Vaccoroni of Italy is one of the favorites for the 1984 Olympic gold medal in the women's foil. Epee and saber—male-only events so far in international competition—have as current world champions, respectively, Elmar Borrmann of West Germany and Vasil Etropolski of Bulgaria.

One of the best U.S. fencers competes in saber. He is Peter Westbrook of New York, gold medalist in the 1983 Pan Am Games and seven-time U.S. champion prior to 1984. The last American to win an individual medal in the Olympics was Albert Axelrod, with a bronze in the 1960 men's foil in Rome, but no American has ever won a gold medal.

Vladimir Romankov of the Soviet Union, five times the men's world foil champion, including the last two years, is determined to win his first Olympic gold medal this year. The 1980 Olympic gold medalist was Soviet teammate Vladimir Smirnov, who was killed by a broken blade during team competition in 1982, a tragic accident that continues to spur debate in the fencing world over the need for more stringent equipment testing and innovative safety measures.

Fencing as a spectator sport is enhanced, no doubt, by the clash of steel and the bravado in this "Western martial art," which is distinctive in that it has no fighting classification by weight or size. Because the blade action is so fast, however, the actual touches are difficult to see. Electronic scoring has been used for several decades in foil and epee to aid the judges and, incidentally, the spectators. To date, no electronic system has been officially approved for recording the touches in saber fencing.

Foilists and epeeists wear what look like retractable electronic "leashes" fixed to the back of their jackets. Wires extend through their clothing to the hand guard, where a plug connects to a wire running along a groove in the foil and epee blades. When the movable tip of the sword is depressed on a touch, a signal lights up a scoring machine. Because only the torso is a valid target in foil fencing, a metallic-content jacket is worn to distinguish good touches from off-target hits.

Judges (called directors) are essential to regulate the action on the fencing strips, each 14 meters (nearly 46 feet) long and 2 meters (6½ feet) wide. But in foil and saber events, the directors must also determine whether the correct moves were made to establish the attacker's "right of way." If the attacker's blade is parried (warded off) by the opponent's weapon, look for the attacker to go on the defensive immediately to meet the opponent's riposte (the quick thrust after the parry) before trying to assume the offensive again.

Because saber fencing requires the "right of way" sequence and lacks an electronic scoring aid as well, one director and four judges are needed. Directors police the action, judges do the scoring.

After the preliminary rounds, the fencing bouts for men have twelve-minute time limits and for women ten-minute time limits. Men have a goal of 10 touches, women 8. The winner has to have a 2-point margin of victory, however, unless the men become tied at 12-12 and the women at 10-10. Then the first fencer to score a clean touch wins. If the time limit expires without either fencer getting 10 (or 8) points, the score is advanced to the maximum amount, keeping the same lead that existed when time expired. Thus, a male fencer leading 8-5 after twelve minutes would be declared a 10-7 winner. The final scores, therefore, might not indicate the actual touches during the bout.

In the 1983 men's epee final at the U.S. championships, for instance, Paul Pesthy and Tim Glass were extra-cautious, neither scoring a touch during regulation time. Their scores were advanced to the maximum, 12-12, with only one touch now required to win. A mere twenty seconds into the "sudden death" overtime, Pesthy slipped in his epee point to Glass's chest and got the victory.

Women have been fencing in the
Olympics for 60 years, but when they
started, the uniform of the day was
somewhat conservative. Here a fencer of
the Roaring Twenties poses demurely.
Photo by Carroll Photo Service

Attacking Italian Angelo Scuri defeated
Vitali Loguine, U.S.S.R., to help win the
gold medal in team foil at the World
University Games in Canada in July, 1983.
AP Laserphoto

Two fencers go at it with epees, one of the three Olympic forms. Photo by David Madison/Focus on Sports

Wrestling action from the 1982 Amateur World Cup—U.S.A. vs. U.S.S.R. Photo by Kishimoto Corp.

Inset: Japanese wrestler Hideaki Tomiyama gets on top. Photo by Kishimoto Corp.

Above: American weightlifter Jeff Michels. Photo by Focus on Sports. *Below:* Chinese lifter Wu Shude s a world-class competitor in the 123-pound division. Photo by Baseball Magazine-sha

Super-heavyweight Anatoli Pisarenko of U.S.S.R. looks good for Olympic gold. Photo by Chuck Muhlstock/

U.S. and Dominican Republic boxers square off in the 1983 North American Boxing Championships. Photos by Bob

Lachman/*Los Angeles Times*

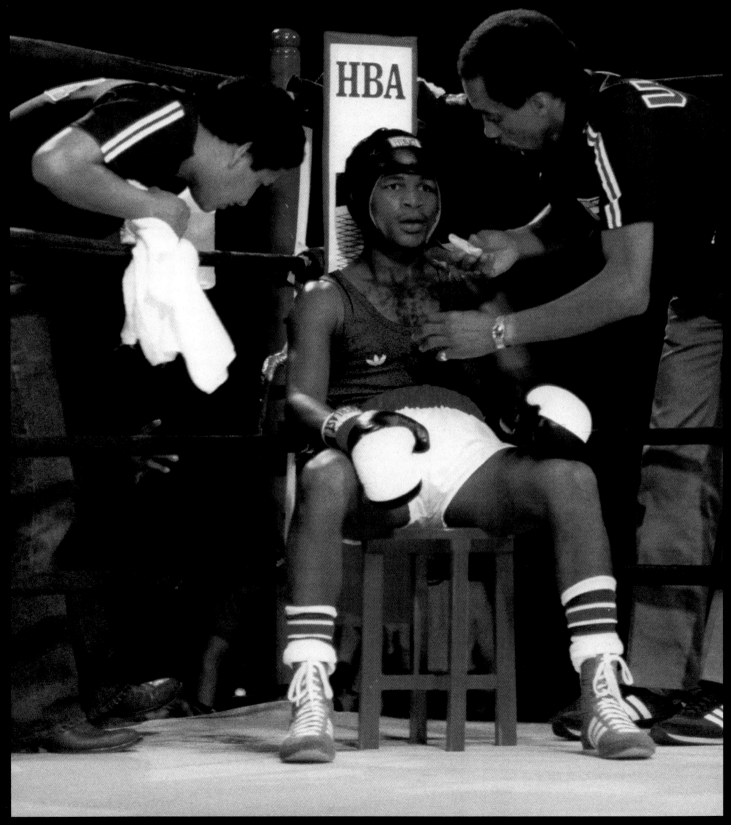

Veteran cornermen, a superior coach in Pat Nappi and new full-time training facilities in Colorado Springs support the U.S. boxing team. Photo by Bob Lachman/*Los Angeles Times*

BOXING

BY EARL GUSTKEY

It always has been, of course, the most important amateur boxing tournament in the world. But this time, there's something at stake besides medals. Money. Lots of it.

Go ahead. Dream along with America's (and Canada's, and Italy's...) Olympic boxing hopefuls. Dream along, about what would happen if:

■ Welterweight Mark Breland of New York City, already a world amateur champion, is a sensation at the Los Angeles Olympics. He beats everyone he boxes and wins the gold medal. Already there's talk of a one-year, $2 million contract for Breland if he wins the gold.

■ Super-heavyweight Tyrell Biggs of Philadelphia meets Teofilo Stevenson, the Cuban legend, in the Olympic final before sixteen thousand wildly cheering Americans and untold millions around the world on television. Biggs knocks Stevenson kicking. Okay, now you're talking about real dough.

■ Light-flyweight Paul Gonzales of East Los Angeles does the same, finishing up in the final with a dramatic knockout of a Cuban world champion, Rafael Sainz. With one million-plus Hispanics in Los Angeles County, Gonzales could use his Olympic gold medal and toothpaste smile to catapult himself into the same income bracket as the Dodgers' Fernando Valenzuela.

■ A Canadian heavyweight named Willie de Wit flattens everyone, including the Soviet Union's national champion, Alexander Yagubkin. Drumroll, curtain, lights: And here he is, boxing fans, your Great White Hope heavyweight.

Remember, Sugar Ray Leonard was a boxing sensation at the 1976 Montreal Olympics. When he turned pro, he earned $40,000 for his first fight. Two years ago, Canadian light-middleweight Shawn O'Sullivan was offered $100,000 to turn pro, two years before the Olympics. O'Sullivan is still an amateur, one of the world's best, and will also be standing in the cashier's line at Los Angeles. Breland said he turned down an offer of $500,000 to turn pro in the spring of 1982. Obvious question: What's he worth as an Olympic champion?

So in the context of this Olympic boxing tournament, set aside the ideals of international sporting brotherhood, the pure values of Olympic competition and all the other malarkey about how wonderful amateur sports are, about how important it is simply to take part. This is a money tournament. Here's to the win-

ners. Champagne toasts. It's contract time. For gold medalists from Western countries, you're looking at some very big paydays. The track record for Olympic boxing champions vaulting into professional ranks for significantly more money than they would have otherwise commanded begins in 1976 with Leonard, the Olympic light-welterweight champion that year and later world pro welterweight champion. Compare Leonard's $40,000 for his first pro bout to Aaron Pryor, who didn't make the 1976 Olympic team and got $100 for his first. In 1952, a couple of months after Floyd Patterson won the Olympic middleweight gold medal, he pocketed $75 for his first pro bout. Muhammad Ali, after winning the light-heavyweight gold medal in 1960, made $2,000 for his first pro appearance, in Louisville, Kentucky, his hometown.

But by 1976, the stakes were much higher for two reasons:

■ Huge television exposure.

■ The 1976 Olympics took place in North America.

Without doubt, boxing champions from Western nations will become the wealthiest athletes to emerge from the Los Angeles Olympics, where television coverage will dwarf all previous Olympics, and where boxers will be performing before enthusiastic, flag-waving, pro-American crowds for thirteen days. Endorsement, marketing and promotion contracts and the commercial and satellite television networks that bind it all together provide a world-class boxer of today with the opportunity to earn sums of money unimaginable a generation ago. Case in point: Rocky Marciano, boxing's biggest gate attraction of the 1950s, left boxing a millionaire, yet never earned more than $482,000 for a single bout. Sugar Ray Leonard, in 1981, earned $10 million for one fight, the Tommy Hearns bout. And within a decade, some have predicted, the growth of pay-for-view television systems will have reached the point where a highly attractive pro boxing match could generate revenues in excess of $100 million.

And Americans won't have a monopoly on rich Olympic champions. An Italian sportswriter said of Francesco Damiani, a 1984 gold medal super-heavyweight candidate from Italy: "An Olympics gold medal for Damiani would make him an instant millionaire." The same is said of De Wit, the twenty-two-year-old Canadian heavyweight with the big knockout punch.

Amateur boxing is the sport in which combatants wear black and white gloves, tank-top shirts and headgear, and seemingly put themselves at the

mercy of judges and referees who—to the uninitiated and even to some seasoned observers—appear to know nothing about boxing.

Every four years, pro boxing followers work themselves into a fury watching Olympic boxing. They have no patience for referees who seem to meddle in the ebb and flow of a bout and make strange decisions. Viewers weaned on pro boxing need to be reprogrammed before settling in to follow Olympic boxing at the Los Angeles Sports Arena. It is, in fact, a different sport.

Here are some major differences between amateur and pro boxing:

■ All bouts are three rounds.

■ There are twelve weight classes, from light-flyweight (105 pounds) to super-heavyweight (over 201).

■ Glove sizes, which in pro boxing vary around the world and from state to state, are standardized in international boxing. In the six lightest weight classes, boxers wear eight-ounce gloves; ten-ounce gloves are used in the six heaviest classes.

■ Three knockdowns in one round or four in one bout end the match. In addition, three standing eight-counts in one round or four in one bout end the contest.

■ The referee is in full control, more so than his pro counterpart. He'll commonly interrupt the action to caution boxers for fouls such as holding, employing a passive defense (covering up with both hands), not stepping back when ordered to break and head butting.

■ Judging is done by five judges. An effort is made to provide an international mix for each bout. If an American is boxing an East German, for example, the judges might include a Venezuelan, a Japanese, a Canadian, a Pole and a Hungarian.

■ Judges are backed by a jury of from three to five others who also score the bout. If the front line judges score a bout 3-2, the jury's scorecards are tabulated before a decision is announced. The jury can overrule the front line judges, but only if it votes the other way by 5-0 or 4-1.

■ A scoring blow is registered when the white area of the glove—the knuckle area—lands cleanly to the head or body. A knockdown punch is scored the same as a cleanly delivered jab, and points are also awarded to a boxer who skillfully slips punches.

Boxing spectators oriented to the pros have difficulty with amateur scoring. But amateur boxing scores a knockdown punch the same as a jab for two reasons: it is believed that the rule encourages the development of complete boxing skills and, most important, it results in safer bouts. Since 1945, according to *Ring* magazine, there have been slightly more than 350 deaths in pro boxing. A figure for international amateur boxing in the same period is difficult to find, but the U.S.A. Amateur Boxing Federation says it's aware of only five U.S. deaths and two serious injuries in the last ten years, in over 750,000 bouts.

Amateur boxers are trained, coached and taught to win by rolling up points with jabs, counterpunches and defensive skills. That doesn't mean, however, that amateur boxing doesn't have its share of crowd-pleasing, wade-in slugger types. Canada's Willie de Wit and the U.S.'s Ricky Womack come quickly to mind. Nevertheless, the scoring system favors the skillful boxer who possesses a consistent jab, is quick afoot and avoids excessive punishment over a thirteen-day tournament, a boxer like the U.S.'s Breland. In long tournaments, brawlers may become so battered by the semifinals that they can hardly crawl out of their Olympic Village beds in the morning, let alone compete effectively. Further, all-around boxers often avoid the hand injuries so common in amateur tournaments. A dependable, high-scoring jab and only an occasional scoring right is a safer strategy than a greater abundance of punches with greater velocity. Punches that land on the opponent's arms or shoulders are nonscoring blows and in fact may result in defensive points for the opponent. Says Gonzales, a light-flyweight favorite in the Olympics: "In a long boxing tournament, everyone's hands get beat up, swollen and sore. You're better off if you throw punches that count."

Like American athletes in other Olympic sports—swimming and track and field, to name two—some U.S. boxers may encounter tougher competition at the Olympic trials than at the Olympics. In America, as Pat Nappi, U.S. Olympic boxing coach, likes to say, "the talent well is very deep in some weight classes."

In the bantamweight class (119 pounds), for example, the Olympic team berth is a tossup among five boxers: Todd Hickman (Akron, Ohio); Floyd Favors (Capitol Heights, Maryland); Jesse Benavides (Corpus Christi, Texas); Michael Collins (LaPorte,

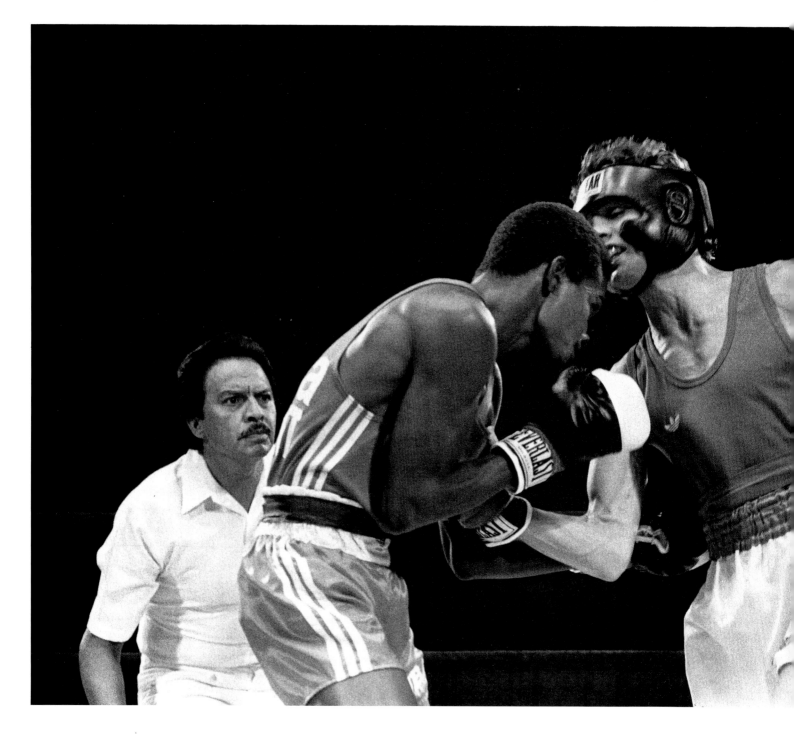

Texas); and Ronnie Rentz (Albuquerque, New Mexico). In the welterweights, Louis Howard of St. Louis would be favored by some to win the Olympic championship, but he has a problem. He's in the same weight class as Breland.

In the months before the Olympics, the top favorites to make the U.S. Olympic team were Gonzales (106 pounds); Pernell Whitaker, from Norfolk, Virginia (132); Breland (147); Womack, from Detroit (178); and Biggs (super-heavyweight). Breland and Biggs looked like sure bets: Breland, the world champion welterweight, is considered the best amateur in the world; Biggs had a 3-0 career mark against America's second-best super-heavyweight, Craig Payne of Livonia, Michigan.

And what of America's overall chances for success in Los Angeles? In the days before the L.A. Olympics, standards of success for the U.S. boxing team will be measured against "the team the stars fell on," the 1976 U.S. juggernaut that won five gold medals at Montreal, same as the 1952 U.S. Olympic team. Nappi coached the 1976 team, too, and if he thinks that kind of talent is around today, he wasn't committing himself in the early months of 1984. "It's too early to say," he said. "I'm not even sure who's going to be on our team, let alone who they'll be boxing against in Los Angeles."

Other U.S. amateur boxing officials were similarly reserved. But Loring Baker, U.S.A./A.B.F. president, said, "The United States has five amateur world champions. How many other countries have that many?" The answer is none.

Favors, Breland and Biggs all won world titles at the 1982 world championship tournament in Munich, so there are at least three Americans who've shown they can go the distance in an Olympic-caliber tournament with the best in the world. And win. On March 18, 1983, in Reno, in a one-night world champion "box-off," Steve McCrory (112) took a world title away from Yuri Alexandrov of the Soviet Union on a 3-2 decision, and Pernell Whitaker decisioned two-time Olympic champion and world champion Angel Herrera of Cuba, 5-0.

Five world champions. For Americans looking ahead to the Olympics, it seems like a nice round figure.

Left: *Andrew Minsker* (right), *from Milwaukie, Oregon, is among ranking U.S. featherweights. Here, he delivers a body blow to Cuba's Jesus Sollet. Photo by Bob Lachman*/Los Angeles Times

Above: *Craig Payne (right), U.S. super-heavyweight, throws a right hand on his way to an upset over the Cuban legend Teofilo Stevenson at the 1983 North American championships.*

Opposite: *Payne (right) becomes one of the few boxers ever to have his hand raised in victory over Stevenson. Photos by Bob Lachman/Los Angeles Times*

Above: *Mark Breland, a welterweight, is considered by many the hottest prospect in amateur boxing.*

Left: *Pernell Whitaker, U.S.A., swarms over Angel Beltre to win a lightweight match decision at the Pan Am Games in August, 1983. AP Laserphoto*

WRESTLING

BY DAVE DISTEL

To many Americans, the greatest wrestlers have names like Andre the Giant, Gorgeous George and Dick the Bruiser. In fact, the greatest wrestlers are those whose names often appear in the smallest type at the bottom of the sports results page in the morning newspaper. These fellows are the amateurs, and they wrestle in much the same way the Greeks wrestled in the ancient Olympic games. Wrestling was part of the pentathlon in those centuries B.C., and there have been few changes since in this most elemental human combat.

"Wrestling," said freestyler Chris Campbell, the strongest U.S. Olympic hopeful at 180.5 pounds, "is like a chess match. It's all moves and countermoves, just you and the other guy on the mat."

And the moves are basic at the same time that they are intricate.

"There are an infinite number of moves," said Dan Gable, the U.S. freestyle coach. "I'm thirty-five and I've been close to the sport for twenty-five years, but I continue to learn. Every time I go to the world championships, I see several varieties or variations I'd never seen before. You can never stop learning."

Gable, the Olympic freestyle champion at 149.5 pounds in Munich in 1972, is probably the best-known name in U.S. amateur wrestling—in part because of his success as a competitor and in part because of his success as a coach. He has coached the University of Iowa to the last six NCAA championships and eight in the last nine years.

Freestyle, as the name implies, is what might be called the no-holds-barred form of international wrestling—hands and arms, legs and feet. Kind of an anything-goes approach. The U.S. has enjoyed most of its success in freestyle, though it will likely trail the Soviet Union in medals won in Los Angeles.

The other form of Olympic wrestling is Greco-Roman, but the U.S. has done poorly in international competition in this form. No holds are allowed below the waist in Greco-Roman. Hands and arms do their work against hands and arms.

In the U.S., freestyle is the more popular because it is easier to make the transition from interscholastic and intercollegiate rules to international freestyle rules. "There's still a big difference," Gable said. "We emphasize control, whereas international rules deempha-size control and emphasize spectacular situations. They seem to be more interested in a show." Internationally, for example, a wrestler gets maximum points for executing a maneuver known as a "grand amplitude," a spectacular move that entails lifting an opponent into the air and slamming him to the mat. "Under our collegiate rules," Gable said, "that move is illegal."

But U.S. wrestlers adapt. Campbell, the 180.5-pounder from Iowa State, was kiddingly nicknamed "Cosmonaut Campbell" by the Russians when he was unceremoniously tossed in the air in a Soviet meet. Campbell did not care for the kidding, however; he returned the favor to the USSR's Teymuraz Dzgoev to win the 1983 World Cup gold medal.

Afterward, Gable said: "Go ask Dzgoev how it feels to be a cosmonaut."

Campbell is one of perhaps three U.S. wrestlers considered by Gable to have a chance to win a gold medal in 1984. However, Campbell did not compete in the 1983 world championships, in part because of a lingering back injury and in part because of pre-law studies. He has moved from Ames, Iowa, to Iowa City to be closer to Gable at the University of Iowa. Campbell, now twenty-eight, said, "The only reason I'm still wrestling is because I want to have a chance to compete in the Olympics."

Gable's other "best bets" are Lee Kemp, from the University of Wisconsin, and Dave Schultz, from Oklahoma State. The catch is that both wrestlers compete at 163 pounds. Kemp's postgraduate studies in marketing took him out of the 1983 world championships, and Schultz won.

The dilemma encountered by Campbell and Kemp—choosing priorities between studies and competition—is virtually nonexistent in the Soviet Union. "Once one of our people has been dominant and won maybe a world championship or an Olympic medal," Gable said, "they retire because they have to earn a living. In the Soviet Union, wrestling *is* their profession."

As examples, Gable could have used himself and Alexander Medved, a Soviet wrestler who won three Olympic gold medals and seven world championships in an eleven-year period from 1962 to 1972. Gable won the 1971 world championship and the 1972 gold medal, then quit to go into coaching. "In Russia," he said, "I probably would have been wrestling until 1980."

Ivan Yarygin, Soviet freestyle coach, conceded that wrestling gets more support in his country. "We have sports schools in the USSR for our children," he said. "In fact, many of our boys start wrestling when they are ten years old.

We've had cases when sixteen-year-olds won world championships."

Soviet wrestlers are difficult to peg because Yarygin is evasive when asked to evaluate his team. However, the Brothers Beloglazov—114.5-pound Anatoli and 125.5-pound Sergei—have each won three world or Olympic championships. Arsen Fadzaev, at 149.5 pounds, was the dominant winner in the 1983 world championships, and Salman Khasimikov continues to roll along as the world's least-known heavyweight champion.

"It's hard to say who will be on our Olympic team," exlplained Anatoli Beloglazov, "because we'll all probably be meeting four or five equal competitors in our national championships." That kind of tough competition also exists in Bulgaria, Japan and Romania, the other top wrestling countries.

Soviet fans and fans in those other countries will know a great deal about those national championships. No Andre the Giants or Dick the Bruisers to confuse them.

Left: *Dan Gable, who was America's most famous amateur wrestler when he won a gold medal in 1972, returns to the Olympics as coach of the U.S. freestyle wrestling team. The photo shows Gable as he was in the early 1970s. Photo by Los Angeles Times*

Below: *Bantamweight Sergei Beloglazov trips up Mongolian Dugarsuren Ouinabold to take the gold medal in 1980.*
AP Wirephoto

Right: *Lee Kemp from Chardon, Ohio, will wrestle his countryman Dave Schultz, the world champion at 163 pounds, for a spot on the U.S. freestyle wrestling team. AP Wirephoto*

Below: *Light-heavyweight Frank Andersson of Sweden topples Greece's George Pozidis in a Greco-Roman match at Moscow. Andersson was fourth overall; Pozidis eighth. AP Wirephoto*

WEIGHTLIFTING

BY CHRIS BAKER

Traditionally in the sport of weightlifting, super-heavyweights such as 360-pound Vasily Alexeyev of the Soviet Union have received most of the attention. But a couple of compactly built Bulgarian teen-agers named Naim Suleimanov and Stefan Topurov may be changing that at the 1984 Olympics in L.A.

Suleimanov, age sixteen, 4-foot-11, 123 pounds, is on the verge of lifting triple body weight in the clean and jerk. He set a world record of 352.5 pounds last year at the Recordmakers Meet in Allentown, Pennsylvania. Topurov, nineteen, became the world's first athlete to put three times his body weight overhead. Competing in the 132-pound class at the world championships in Moscow last October, Topurov lifted 396 pounds in the clean and jerk. Weightlifting experts were stunned. "I didn't think it would happpen so soon," said Herb Glossbrenner, the official statistician for the U.S. Weightlifting Federation. "I didn't think it would happen until the 1984 Olympics."

Harvey Newton, U.S. Olympic coach, said, "In 1976, weightlifting had Alexeyev at the Olympics and gymnastics had Nadia and parents wanted their little girls to be gymnasts. But they didn't want their sons to become weightlifters because they thought you had to look like Alexeyev."

The new breed of weightlifter is, indeed, lighter and more efficient. Super-heavyweight Anatoli Pisarenko, twenty-seven, the Bull of Kiev, weighs almost 90 pounds less than Alexeyev did, but he has surpassed all of Alexeyev's great lifts.

Weightlifting has come a long way since the 1896 Olympics in Athens, when it was part of the track and field competition. Then, there were only two lifts, the dumbbell and the barbell. Legend has it that Prince George of Greece, one of the judges, stole the show from the lifters at Athens. When one of the loaders had trouble removing a weight, Prince George, 6 feet 5 and powerfully built, picked up one of the heavier weights and threw it out of the way.

The first official Olympic weightlifting competition was held at the 1920 Olympics in Antwerp. There were five weight classes then (there are ten today). Belgium won the first team championship, followed by Italy (1924), Germany (1928), France (1932) and Egypt (1936). The U.S. dominated weightlifting after World War II, winning three straight Olympic team championships from 1948 to 1956. But the U.S. hasn't won a gold medal since 1960, and the Soviet Union and Eastern Bloc countries now dominate the sport. Things are not expected to improve this year. The Soviet Union has won every Olympic team championship since 1960, although Bulgaria is closing the gap.

There used to be three Olympic lifts—the press, the snatch and the clean and jerk. The press was eliminated after the 1972 Olympics because some officials felt it was too easy for the lifters to cheat.

Each nation may enter a total of ten lifters, but no more than two per weight class. Final placement is based on the weight total of the two lifts—snatch and clean and jerk. Only the best successful lift is used in figuring the final total. In the case of a tie, the lighter lifter is declared the winner. A lifter has three chances to successfully complete each lift. If a lifter misses on all three lifts, he is eliminated from the competition. That is called bombing out. Three referees judge the competition. To be successful, a lift must receive a minimum of two affirmative votes. The votes are indicated by lights—white for a good lift and red for no lift. A jury of three other referees observes the judges to ensure impartiality.

The two-hand snatch is the first lift. It must be done in one continuous movement, with the bar moving from the floor to an overhead position as the lifter bends or splits his legs and thrusts the bar up. It must remain there until the referee's signal to lower the bar. The referee's signal can't be given until the lifter is virtually motionless.

The clean and jerk is a two-part lift. First, the bar is lifted from the floor to the chest in one motion. Then it is lifted overhead while the lifter dips under the bar. At the conclusion of the jerk, the lifter must stand motionless until the referee's signal.

Each lifter has two minutes in which to get onto the platform and lift the bar past the knees. A warning buzzer sounds at the one-minute mark. The order of the lifters is decided by requesting beginning weight. If two lifters request the same opening weight, they draw lots to see who goes first. Between the first and second lifts, the weight must be increased by a minimum of 5 kilograms. After the second successful lift, the weight must be increased by 2.5 kilograms. The only time it may be increased by less is if the lifter is going for a world record; all world records must be broken by a minimum of one-half kilogram.

The United States's chances of winning a weightlifting medal at the 1984 Olympics are extremely slim, especially if heavyweight Jeff Michels, the national champion, remains ineligible. Michels was banned for two years after he was caught with an illegal level of testosterone in his system at the Pan American Games last summer. Bans of this sort are occasionally lifted, or shortened in duration. The entire U.S. team of seven lifters failed to complete one or both of the required lifts at the world championships.

U.S. lifters with longshot possibilities include Ken Clark of Pacifica, California, Curt White of St. Louis and Rich Winter of Chicago. Among the top world lifters are world champions Blagoi Blagoev and Asen Zlatev of Bulgaria and Pisarenko of the Soviet Union.

One of the great stories in weightlifting is that of 132-pound featherweight Yoshinobu Miyake of Japan, who took gold medals in 1964 and 1968, setting or equaling world and Olympic records with evey lift but one. Miyake's brother Yoshiyuki joined him on the medal platform with a bronze in 1968. The elder Miyake competed again in 1972 and placed fourth in his division. Photo by Kishimoto Corp.

In the World Cup weightlifting championships at Tokyo in December, 1983, Soviet heavyweight Alexander Korlovich had a total of 440 kilograms, giving him a win in his division. *Photo by Kishimoto Corp.*

Flyweight North Korean Han-Gyong Si only took a bronze medal at the 1980 Moscow Olympics because his body weight was higher than the Soviet athlete who lifted the same total in three tries. On a permitted fourth, Si raised 113 kilograms (248.6 pounds) for a new world record in the clean and jerk. *AP Wirephoto*

JUDO

BY DICK RORABACK

It is a philosophy, a contest, a ritual, an exercise in pure physics. It is a tooth-chipping, arm-shattering, knock-down-drag-out brawl. It is the sport of judo, a sport named for a Japanese word that translates as "the gentle way."

The question is, "gentle" compared to what? To a midnight mugging, perhaps. As the only martial art certified as sport in the modern Olympic era, judo holds its own, and then some, with the most explosive of contact competitions.

Nevertheless, what is a martial art doing in the Olympics in the first place?

The answer is a tribute to Jigoro Kano, who "invented" the sport in Japan in the 1880s. A sickly youth, Kano built himself up in body, mind and spirit through intense practice of the military arts of his time. Kano set out to eliminate the more deadly aspects of Asian martial arts, synthesizing from them two relatively wholesome physical exercises: jujitsu, originally practiced by peaceful but pragmatic monks to ward off pillagers, includes hand and foot blows; judo, more sport than self-defense, concentrates on throwing and grappling techniques.

In the lexicon of fighting arts, then, judo is a "soft" as opposed to a "hard" discipline. The latter involves force opposed by force. The former uses incoming force against itself to defeat the attacker. In the modern version of judo, players (judokas) wear *gi,* a loose-fitting garment providing an infinite number of grabholds, and three major tactics are employed to win a match quickly, decisively and often painfully.

The first is the throw, a combination of strength, physics and surprise. When executed perfectly—which is rare but spectacular—the opponent will hurtle through the air and crash on his back, effectively ending the match. Even the neophyte will immediately recognize the maneuver, invariably accompanied by a full-throated roar from the crowd. At the international level, however, competitors are so evenly matched in both strength and savvy that a clean throw is unusual. Opponents, who have begun the match in a standing position, most often go down to the mat locked together, grappling furiously to gain position for one of the other two major tactics.

Another is the chokehold, which involves grasping the lapels of an opponent's *gi* and applying pressure to the neck, eventually resulting in unconsciousness unless the opponent gives up by tapping with his hand. If neither hand is free, a foot tap signals submission. Referees, incidentally, are trained to watch for the feet going limp; advanced black-belt holders, moreover, are schooled in resuscitation techniques. In major competitions, as U.S. team manager Jim Wolley notes, "You'll never see them give up; they'd just as soon be choked unconscious."

The third major tactic is the arm bar or arm lock, which, carried to its logical conclusion, would result in a broken limb. In theory, the referee will signal the end of a match when a judoka's position seems untenable. In practice, the judoka caught in an arm lock will endure. In fact, Jimmy Martin, six-time national champion and an arm-bar specialist, recalls being beaten on decision by a Soviet opponent whose arm he had shattered only moments before. Any of the three maneuvers will result in an *ippon,* or full point, and victory. So will any hold that immobilizes the opponent for a full thirty seconds.

Often, however, the match will be decided on partial scores, awarded by the referee and/or two judges during the match. Partial scores are called *wazari, yuko* and *koka,* in descending order, though judo initiates can fully enjoy the competition without comprehending the foreign terms. The referee will also signal partial scores with arm movements somewhat similar to semaphore. In general, the higher the arm is held, the higher the score—*ippon* if straight up, *wazari* (roughly half a point) to the side, etc.

Japanese is the international language of judo, and familiarity with, and practice of, judo decreases with the distance west from Japan—though the rest of the world is catching on fast. It is estimated that 12 million people are involved in organized judo, two-thirds of them in Japan. Judokas in South Korea and the Soviet Union, both major Olympic threats, number in the hundreds of thousands. The French (500,000), English and Italians will field strong teams, while in the U.S., some 100,000 athletes practice judo, half of them competitively.

If the American Olympic pool is relatively shallow, hampered until recently by lack of funds and publicity, it is bolstered by enthusiasm, dedication and hope, a hope that is not entirely unfounded. In the Tokyo Games of 1964, the first year in which judo was an Olympic sport, Japanese were stunned by the victory in the open division of Anton Geesink, a Dutchman. Of great significance to the American judo movement was the bronze medal won in the middleweight division by Jim Bregman. Since then, the feat has been equaled by Allen Coage in 1972 in Munich, but never bettered. In 1964 one of the members of the U.S. team was Paul Maruyama, a scrappy young lightweight. Maruyama, a lieutenant colonel in the Air Force and now coach of the U.S. Olympic team, has reason to hope that the 1984 crop of American judokas may well surpass the modest glory of their pioneering predecessors.

U.S. Judo Inc., the new national governing body, has unified operation of the sport, helped provide training of a caliber unheard of before the 1980s and afforded promising athletes the opportunity to compete in all parts of the world.

From among them have emerged judokas of real promise for 1984: Leo White, an army lieutenant from Monterey, California, who competes in the 209-pound division; Bobby Berland, a splendid stylist from Wilmette, Illinois, and San Jose State, who placed third at 189 pounds in the 1983 world championships in Moscow; Dewey Mitchell of Seven Springs, Florida, who played football for Bear Bryant at Alabama and competes in judo's open division. Middleweight Mike Swain, lightweight Ed Liddie, heavyweight Miguel Tudela and three or four others have excellent chances not only to gain one of the eight berths on the American team but to make Olympic inroads. The competition, as usual, will come mainly from Japan, the Soviet Union and South Korea.

American senior men's judo combatants are beside themselves at the nationals in 1983. The U.S. has captured only two medals, a silver and a bronze, since the sport was introduced at the 1964 Olympics in Tokyo. Photo by Rick Meyer/ Los Angeles Times

Brent Barron, a top man in the U.S. 172-pound division, flips Nick Price and goes on to win a first round in the 1983 nationals. He lost the final to Robert Patteson, but took a gold in the Pan Am Games. Photo by Rick Meyer/ Los Angeles Times

First-class Japanese judo athlete Yasuhiro Yamashita at the All Japan tournament. Photo by Kishimoto Corp.

Flying Dutchman-type boats compete for places on the U.S. Olympic team. Photo by Ken Hively/*Los Angeles Times*

Top college rowers at the Pac-10 Championships. Photo by David Madison/Focus on Sports

Top: U.S. women's eight took a silver medal at the world championships in August, 1983. Photo by Brian Hill, courtesy U.S. Rowing Association. *Above:* Wet action from the 1976 Olympics. Photo by Royden Hobson/Focus on Sports

American medal prospect Mary T. Meagher leaps out front for a 200-meter freestyle swim.
Photos by Dave Gatley/*Los Angeles Times*

Top: U.S. sprinter Rowdy Gaines.   *Above:* Soviet distance swimmer Sviatoslav Semenov. Photos by Dave Gatley/ *Los Angeles Times*

A fast start in the women's 100-meter backstroke at the Olympic pool. Photo by Dave Gatley/*Los Angeles Times*

Two first-rate Soviet swimmers: (top), Gennadi Utenkov in the 4 x 100-meter medley relay; (above), Vladimir Shemetov

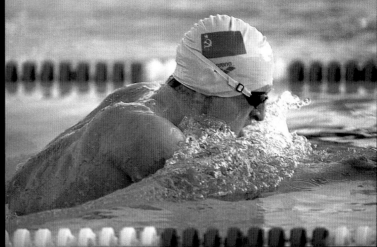

backstroke specialist. Photos by Dave Gatley/*Los Angeles Times*

In the first-ever synchronized swimming competition in the Olympics, U.S. duet team Candy Costie and Tracie Ruiz look good for gold. Photos by Con Keyes/*Los Angeles Times*

Above left: Wendy Wyland works well off the 10-meter platform.   *Above right:* American diver Greg Louganis is at the top

of the field in both springboard and platform diving. Photos by Dave Gatley/*Los Angeles Times*

By mid-July, 1983, a full year before the Games, U.S. diver Megan Neyer was in good form. Photo by Dave Gatley/
Los Angeles Times

DIVING

BY JOHN WEYLER

World-class divers combine strength, coordination and pure athletic prowess with a poise and balletic grace that make them special among Olympic athletes.

Greg Louganis, twenty-four, of Mission Viejo, California, considered by many to be the finest diver of all time, says of his sport: "I look at diving as something musical. I don't want it to be structured. I like it to be esthetic."

In diving, beauty and grace are the most important qualities. But despite the apparent ease of execution by the world's best, diving is not easy to master. Unlike most sports, it is not based on natural skills acquired in childhood, such as running, throwing or bouncing a ball.

"Everything must be learned from scratch," said Ron O'Brien, United States Olympic diving coach. "Sure, much of it is related to gymnastics, but it's much easier to learn to come down on your feet than it is to land head first. It's just not natural."

Obviously, courage is a necessity. A 10-meter platform diver hits the water at more than 30 m.p.h. and a mistimed entry can result in an embarrassingly painful flop, or a serious injury.

High diving evolved over the centuries, stemming from the pastimes of Polynesians and Mexicans who were adept at diving from the tops of waterfalls into pools or off cliffs into the ocean.

Fancy diving, as dives with somersaults or twists were known for many years, began in Sweden and Germany early in the nineteenth century during the great gymnastic movement in those countries. In the summer, gymnasts moved to the beaches and performed acrobatics over the water.

Until that time, most diving took the form of the simple forward header with the body held straight and the arms extended sideways. That was known in Europe as the Swedish swallow and later in the U.S. as the swan dive.

Springboard diving got international notice when it became a men's event in the 1904 Olympic Games in St. Louis. (The Olympic springboard competition now is on a board three meters above the water. Platform diving from a 10-meter board was added at the 1908 Olympics in London. Women's diving received slower acceptance. Plain high diving was included in the 1912 Games in Stockholm, and the first Olympic women's springboard competition was in 1920 in Antwerp. Not until 1928 in Amsterdam was fancy high diving added for women.

Sweden and Germany dominated diving in the early years, but when World War I halted competition in Europe, the U.S. moved ahead and dominated the sport for the next half-century. Americans won all but five gold medals between 1920 and 1964.

The rest of the world began to catch up, though, and the Americans hit bottom in the 1972 Olympics in Munich when Micki King won the only gold medal for the U.S., in the women's springboard event. Italy's Klaus Dibiasi, often called the best ever before Louganis, won platform titles in the 1968 (Mexico City), 1972 and 1976 (Montreal) Olympics and was the toast of the diving world.

Despite serious challenges from the Soviet and Chinese teams, O'Brien believes, the 1984 U.S. Olympic team will be the strongest since the 1960s. Louganis is close to a shoo-in for a gold on the springboard (he has won recent international springboard events by unprecedented margins) and also is a favorite in the platform competition. Megan Neyer (springboard) and Wendy Wyland (platform) are both world champions. Like Louganis, they train under O'Brien.

Louganis's main competition should come from Sergei Kusman and Alexander Portnov of the Soviet Union and Li Kong Cheng of China in the springboard event, and from American Bruce Kimball and China's Tong Hui and Li Hong Ping in the platform. Three Chinese women—Li Yihua (springboard), Peng Yaunchun (springboard) and Chen Xiao Xia (platform)—have a good chance to win medals, as does Soviet platform diver Alla Lobankina.

Few sports have evolved as fast as diving. Today, youngsters around the world are performing dives considered impossible a few years ago. On September 1, 1982, the International Technical Diving Committee authorized several new, more complex dives.

"When I was diving," O'Brien said, "learning a new dive was a case of Russian roulette. We used to coach each other. Now we take a scientific approach to training and a diver can learn more in a shorter period."

Louganis's strength has stretched the limits of divers throughout the world, who are trying to keep up with the complexity of his dives and the near-flawless quality of his execution.

Part of Louganis's success is a result of his build, a combination of muscular and slim.

"Those long lines are just more pleasing to the eye," O'Brien said. "They make you appear more graceful. The body is the foundation of your score. Take a Greg Louganis dive and put it in another body and you'd have a good score, but it wouldn't be a [perfect] 10."

Olympic contestants must complete a series of dives—some do as few as eight, others as many as eleven, depending on whether it is springboard or platform diving. About half of these are required, half optional. A panel of seven judges rates each dive on a scale of 0 to 10, with the highest and lowest scores being eliminated. The score is then multiplied by the degree of difficulty (every dive has a predetermined degree of difficulty, ranging from 1.2 to 3.5) and the diver with the most points at the end of the competition is the winner.

It may sound simple, but one cannot measure a dive with a yardstick, and judging is highly subjective.

"There are four basic criteria for judging," O'Brien said, "the takeoff, the lift or amount of height acquired, the execution, which includes technique and grace of the dive, and the entry into the water. As it turns out, entry is the great separator, because at this level, the execution is good by all the competitors." The best entry results in little water displacement and perpendicular body position. The latter usually brings the former.

Greg Louganis took a sixth in springboard diving and second off the platform at the 1976 Games; he looks golden in 1984. Photo by Dave Gatley/Los Angeles Times

Bruce Kimball, here doing a backward dive off the 10-meter platform, says it's almost impossible to beat Greg Louganis unless Louganis makes a mistake. When Louganis makes those mistakes, Kimball frequently is the guy who beats him. Photos by Jose Galvez/Los Angeles Times

Wendy Wyland stands as America's best hope for a medal in women's platform diving. Photo by Dave Gatley/Los Angeles Times

SWIMMING

BY ROSS NEWHAN

Swimming was initiated as an Olympic sport at the Athens Games of 1896. Hungary's Alfred Hajos won the first gold medal with a victory in the 100-meter freestyle. Now, eighty-eight years after Hajos plunged into the Bay of Zea near Piraeus, some Olympic swimmers still use a form of the crawl stroke employed by Hajos. But the similarity ends there.

As an Olympic event, swimming has clearly emerged from the crawling stage. The pace and growth of the competition can be measured by the following: Two of the most glamorous personalities in the history of United States swimming, Buster Crabbe and Eleanor Holm, were Olympic stars in the 1932 Games at the Los Angeles Swim Stadium. Crabbe won the 400-meter freestyle in 4 minutes 48.4 seconds. Holm won the 100-meter backstroke in 1:19.4. Neither time would qualify for the 1984 U.S. Olympic team. In fact, neither would qualify for any Olympic team anywhere. Crabbe and Holm would be strictly spectators at the 1984 Games, to be contested in a new, $4 million facility on the USC campus, within splashing distance of the 1932 site.

The Soviet Union's Vladimir Salnikov now holds the world record in the 400-meter freestyle. His time of 3:48.2 is a full minute faster than Crabbe's Olympic time. East Germany's Rica Reinisch now holds the world record in the 100-meter backstroke. Her time of 1:00.86 is almost 19 seconds faster than Holm's Olympic time. Many swimmers now go faster than Crabbe and Holm, which is no disgrace to either's legacy.

Since the discovery of petroglyphs in the Libyan desert traced swimming to at least 4000 B.C., since Hajos battled seaweed and salt water off the coast of Greece, since first Johnny Weissmuller and later Crabbe stepped off an Olympic victory stand and into Tarzan's loincloths, even since 1972, when Mark Spitz won seven gold medals in the Munich Olympics (comparative times indicate he might not win even a bronze in 1984), this is a sport experiencing considerable evolutionary changes.

Consider only this:

The oldest world records among Olympic swimming events date only to 1978, when Australia's Tracey Wickham set marks that are still standing in the 400- and 800-meter freestyles. Among Olympic events, fifteen men's and women's world records were broken in 1983 alone.

Crabbe and Holm were timed by hand-held stopwatches. The new marks are being recorded on electronic devices triggered by the starter's gun and stopped at touch pads hanging from the gutters in each lane. The swimmers setting the records are products of equally sophisticated procedures. They are bigger and stronger. They receive improved coaching, are better trained and learn more competitive techniques. Their drive and ability are honed in a world arena that now finds virtually every continent producing swimmers of gold medal capability.

The 1984 Olympics—on the men's side, at least—will showcase the wide-scale competitiveness and illustrate the difficulty any nation now has in dominating what Don Gambril, the University of Alabama swim coach who is the U.S. Olympic coach, calls "a tougher league now." So tough, in fact, that the U.S. team will come to Los Angeles unsure of even one win in a sport it once ruled. The U.S. men are still formidable, but there seems to be no possibility that they can win all but one event, as they did in the 1976 Games at Montreal, the last Olympic competition for the U.S. Men's teams from the Soviet Union, Canada and East and West Germany now form significant hurdles for the U.S.

And American women confront an even tougher task. In the eight years since 1976, when they emerged from the scientific womb of their intensive and specialized training centers to win all but two events at the Montreal Olympics, the East Germans have made women's swimming their private domain, sweeping or nearly sweeping every major competition. In 1984, they are expected to continue their Olympic dominance.

Reflecting on the shift in world power, Gambril has cited a number of factors. Among them:

■ The cost to parents of keeping a U.S. youth in training for a dozen or more years can be prohibitive, particularly when weighed against the financial opportunities of a professional career in another sport.

■ Exposure to, and participation in, the Olympic movement has made swimming a source of national pride in countries that are comparatively free of professional competition in other sports and are willing to accept the financial obligation of identifying and training young prospects. Some countries go to the extent of finding new jobs for parents who are uprooted and moved closer to national training centers, as well as guaranteeing future employment to fledgling swim stars.

■ The boycott of the 1980 Moscow Olympics deprived the U.S. of a recruiting showcase and left a number of frustrated veterans with neither the spiritual nor financial resources to remain in training for another four years. Many of those who did remain in training have seen the world-best times for their events improved so much that they have had difficulty keeping up.

At the 1982 world championships in Guayaquil, Ecuador, foreign swimmers won twelve of the fifteen women's events and nine of the fifteen men's events. Three of the six wins by U.S. men were in relays.

If all this paints a bleak picture for U.S. hopes in 1984, Gambril sighs and says, "I've been seeing a rejuvenated enthusiasm for some time now. It might not be that bad being in the position of underdog." And Mark Schubert, coach of the successful Mission Viejo, California, Nadadores and an assistant on the Olympic staff, speculates that the U.S. will do better than anticipated because of partisan crowds and home-pool advantage. "We saw how it benefited the Italians in last summer's European championships [in Rome]," Schubert said, referring to Giovanni Franceschi's wins in the 200- and 400-meter individual medleys, each supported by a shrieking, flag-waving crowd.

Among the U.S. swimmers most likely to hear the crowd's roar are:

■ Rick Carey, a University of Texas junior, who set 1983 world records in the 100- and 200-meter backstrokes.

■ Matt Gribble, a University of Miami senior, who set a 1983 world record in the 100-meter butterfly.

■ Steve Lundquist, a Southern Methodist University senior, who set a 1983 world record in the 100-meter breaststroke and had the world's best time in the 200-meter breaststroke.

■ Ambrose (Rowdy) Gaines III, a University of Auburn graduate, who holds the world record in the 100-meter freestyle and held the 200-meter record until the summer of 1983.

■ Tiffany Cohen, a Mission Viejo High School senior, whose 1983 times in the 200-, 400- and 800-meter freestyles were among the world's best.

■ Mary T. Meagher, a former Louisville resident who dropped out of the University of California after her freshman year to prepare for the Olympics at Mission Viejo and who holds the world records in the 100- and 200-meter butterfly.

■ Tracy Caulkins, a University of Florida junior who holds more than forty-five national titles, has been returning to the wunderkind form of her mid-teens and seems a definite medal threat in the individual medleys.

■ Dara Torres, a Mission Viejo High School sophomore who holds the world record in a non-Olympic event, the 50-meter freestyle, and who is now among the world leaders in the 100-meter free-style besides being the leader of a strong U.S. sprint freestyle contingent that includes Texas graduate Jill Sterkel, USC freshman Cynthia Woodhead and Saratoga High School sophomore Carrie Steinseifer.

Among the foreign swimmers likely to make the biggest impression in Los Angeles are:

■ The Soviet Union's Salnikov, probably the greatest distance freestyle swimmer ever and an almost certain gold medalist in the 400- and 1,500-meter freestyles.

■ West Germany's Michael Gross, world record-holder in the 200-meter freestyle and 200-meter butterfly and a gold medal threat in the 100-meter butterfly.

■ Canada's Victor Davis, world record-holder in the 200-meter breast-stroke, and Alex Baumann, world record-holder in the 200-meter individual medley. Baumann also had 1983's world's best time in the 400-meter individual medley, which figures to be one of the most competitive events in the Los Angeles games, pitting Baumann against world record-holder Ricardo Prado of Brazil, Jens-Peter Berndt of East Germany and the impressive Franceschi, among others.

■ East German freestyler Jorge Woithe, backstroker Dirk Richter and a fleet of potential female medalists, including sprint freestylers Birgit Meineke and Kristin Otto; distance free-stylers Astrid Strauss and Anke Sonnenbrodt; backstrokers Ina Kleber, Cornelia Sirch and Birthe Weigang; breaststrokers Ute Geweniger and Sylvia Gerash; butterflyers Ines Geissler and Cornelia Polia; and individual medley performers Petra Schneider, Kathleen Nord and Geweniger.

■ Japan's Hiroko Nagasaki, a fifteen-year-old breaststroker who had the world's best time in the 200 meters in 1983.

A new rule prohibits a country from qualifying more than two swimmers for any final. This will prevent East Germany's women from registering a total medal sweep but will likely not curtail their cornering of the gold and silver market.

The challenge is clear, and Gambril has been preparing for it ever since he began administering the direction of the 1984 Olympic program three years ago. He has, in that time, instituted a series of coaching colleges and developmental summer camps. He has also helped strengthen and enlarge the Junior Olympics. He assigned areas of responsibility to his eight Olympic assistants more than two years ago and has been compiling a dossier on the

strategic habits and techniques of the top foreign swimmers.

The Olympic assignment marks something of a homecoming for Gambril, who attended East Los Angeles Community College and Occidental before getting a degree from Cal State Los Angeles. He has since coached swimming at Rosemead and Arcadia high schools, Pasadena City College, Cal State Long Beach, Harvard and Alabama. He won three national club titles with the Phillips 66 team of Long Beach and another with the City of Commerce swim club. He has produced many world record-holders, Olympic champions and dual-meet titlists. Among the many swim coaches who got their first training as assistants under Gambril are Ron Ballatore of UCLA, Skip Kenney of Stanford, Dick

Jochurns of Arizona and Jay Fitzgerald of the Cincinnati Pepsi-Marlins.

Once, as a teen-ager delivering the *Los Angeles Times* along a fourteen-mile bike route, Don Gambril felt that he would eventually attend a trade school and become a linotype operator. Now, thirty years later, with most newspapers produced by computer and delivered by car, the fifty-two-year-old Gambril returns to Los Angeles as a potential maker of news, rather than a setter of it.

Vladimir Salnikov of the Soviet Union remains the best freestyle swimmer in the world—at distances from 400 to 1,500 meters. Photo by Con Keyes/Los Angeles Times

Right: *Hiroko Nagasaki of Japan, only 14 at the time, won gold medals in the 100-meter and 200-meter breaststroke and set a U.S. Open record at L.A. 83. Photo by Dave Gatley/Los Angeles Times*

Below: *Mary T. Meagher is the fastest female butterfly swimmer of all time, but her best times were achieved in 1981. She ate herself out of world-record class, but now she's on her way back, hoping to peak in L.A. Photo by Con Keyes/Los Angeles Times*

WATER POLO

BY MILES CORWIN

There is high sticking in hockey, hand checking in basketball and the clothesline tackle in football. But the ultimate contact sport may be water polo. It is the only game in which a defensive man literally undresses his opponent. Many players wear two suits because the outer one sometimes is torn off during action.

Water polo appears to be the ideal sport for the stereotypical American fan who enjoys violence and has a short attention span. Players are constantly engaged in mano-a-mano struggles for position, and there is a 35-second shot clock, so spectators are never subjected to prolonged periods of inaction. Yet water polo, which has a tremendous following in Europe, has been largely ignored in the United States. Attendance usually is sparse for international matches, several colleges have dropped water polo in the last few years and corporate sponsorship seems certain to evaporate after the 1984 Olympics.

Monte Nitzkowski, U.S. Olympic water polo coach, is hoping that a strong finish in the 1984 Olympics will generate interest in the sport. "We're going for the gold, but we're also fighting for the survival of our sport," Nitzkowski said. "Having the Olympics in L.A. is a great opportunity to showcase water polo."

The American team should be able to generate interest in the summer of 1984. The players, all Californians, will be performing in their home state; the team operates a crowd-pleasing, fast-paced offense and is a strong contender for a medal. The Olympic site is the ocean-view campus at Pepperdine University in Malibu.

The Soviet Union, which has won the last four international tournaments, including the 1980 Olympics at Moscow, is the gold medal favorite. It is a team without a weakness. It plays superb defense, has the best goalie in the world and plays an extremely versatile offense. It has the size and strength to play a power game, yet also has the speed to score on fast breaks. Traditional water polo powers West Germany, Yugoslavia, Spain, Italy and Hungary are all medal contenders. Although the Hungarian team finished seventh in the major international tournament of 1983, water polo experts expect the team to be a gold medal contender in Los Angeles.

The Hungarians, called by American coaches "the Dallas Cowboys of water

polo," have dominated the international water polo scene for years. Hungarian teams have won a medal in every world championship since 1928 and won six Olympic gold medals, more than any other country. In the 1956 Olympics, the Hungarian team played in the most famous water polo game in history. A month after Soviet tanks rolled into Budapest to crush the Hungarian revolt, the Soviet and Hungarian water polo teams squared off in the Olympic semifinals. More than ten thousand people packed the natatorium in Melbourne, many of them Hungarian expatriates living in Australia, and the game received international press coverage. Throughout the game, players taunted each other, and the water churned with underwater punches and kicks. A Hungarian player was hit on the side of the head and suffered a ruptured eardrum; another was punched above the eye and received eight stitches. Hungary led, 4-0, with several minutes left in the game, but the referee decided to end the match prematurely, before all control was lost.

The U.S. did not place in the 1956 Olympics, and did not win a medal in a post–World War II Olympics until 1972. When Nitzkowski began coaching, the U.S. traditionally was an underdog team at the Olympics. Many European teams were state-supported and played together year-round. U.S team members were scattered throughout California, rarely practiced together and often could not raise the funds to play in international tournaments.

The only way the Americans could do well against the European teams was through innovative tactics. Nitzkowski, water polo coach at Long Beach City College, spent hours on the beach in front of the small restaurant he owns, scratching Xs and Os in the sand, devising a strategy that would enable the U.S. to compensate for its lack of experience and depth. The best water polo teams at the time played a slow, static offense and relied on enormous forwards who looked like pro football defensive ends to power the ball into the goal. Nitzkowski capitalized on the young American team's strong swimming background and devised an offense predicated on speed and endurance. He borrowed strategy from basketball coaches and introduced into the international water polo scene the fast break, pick and roll, a full-court pressing defense and constant counterattacks.

At the 1972 Munich Olympics, Nitzkowski's tactical innovations paid off when the U.S. won a bronze medal. It was the first time since its bronze in 1932 that the U.S. water polo team had

earned a medal in the Olympics. The American team was a crowd favorite in Munich because its mobile, exciting style of play contrasted sharply with the sluggish European teams. German sportswriters called the American offense Space Age Water Polo. Soon, European national coaches were copying Nitzkowski's tactics. After the U.S. team's performance in Munich, it was expected to be a contender for the gold medal in the 1976 Olympics. But the water polo program was chronically short of funds, the Olympic team disbanded and Nitzkowski was replaced as coach. Subsequent national teams were hastily assembled and could not live up to the earlier Olympic success, and the 1976 team failed to qualify for the Games. The 1976 team's failure shook the water polo establishment; money was raised, Nitzkowski was brought back and a year-round national team was formed. The U.S. was ranked second in the world in 1979, and expected to contend for the gold medal in the Moscow Olympics. Then the boycott was announced.

"We were devastated," recalled Steve Hamann, starting goalie on the 1980 national team. "I don't remember if I cried, but I know some guys did. People just don't know how much it hurt.... We'd worked so hard and were so close to that gold medal." Several players retired, and the team spent three years rebuilding. The U.S. team placed fourth in the major international tournament of 1983, won the gold medal at the Pan American Games, and is "on track" for the Olympics, according to Ken Lindgren, assistant Olympic coach. "We lost a lot of momentum after the boycott, but we're making up ground," Lindgren said. "There are three or four teams that could win the gold. We've got to the point where we're one of those teams. I like our chances."

Above: *Soviet goalie E. Sharonov finds he would need Kareem Abdul-Jabbar's reach to block this shot from Holland's Nicolas Landeweerd. The Soviet team, with Sharonov in the net, won the gold in 1980.*
Left: *Italian Marco Baldinetti and Soviet captain Alexander Kabanov get physical in a pre-Olympic tuneup at Malibu in May, 1983. Photos by Con Keyes/* Los Angeles Times

CANOEING

BY BILL CHRISTINE

One of the first times Rudy Helm paddled his kayak at Lake Casitas, he got caught in strong afternoon winds, tried unsuccessfully to avoid a series of waves and was unceremoniously dumped in the water. It wasn't a very smooth introduction to the 1984 Olympic canoeing site for the East German star, who won the gold medal in the 1,000 meters at both Montreal and Moscow.

But for those opponents who think that Helm might be vulnerable in 1984, think again. Helm's test of the Lake Casitas waters was in the middle of the afternoon, when the wind and waves are at their most treacherous; Olympic canoeing events there will be held in the early morning hours, starting around 7 A.M., when the conditions are more favorable. "The winds will be calmer at that earlier hour," said the twenty-eight-year-old Helm, "but the coin has two sides. In order to get ready for the races, I will have to go to bed at eight in the evening and get up around four in the morning. That is not like my usual schedule. I like to stay in bed in the morning."

Several days after his dunking, Helm, who has won the world championship five straight times, stayed dry and won his specialty in the Lake Casitas competition. The countries that finished immediately behind him in the 1983 world championships in Finland didn't compete, but it probably wouldn't have made any difference. Helm's winning margins in the last two world championships have been more than two seconds, which is not indicative of a slowdown. "I've been watching Helm all over the world for the last five years, and I've only seen him lose once," said Terry White, one of America's best kayakers. "Helm is both very strong and technically good. Some have one or the other, but he's got it all."

Helm epitomizes East Germany's recent rise to prominence in canoeing, which has been an Olympic sport since 1936. Events have changed through the years, but in competitions that are still being held, men from the Soviet Union have won seventeen gold medals, more than double the number of any other country, and in 1972 the Soviets finished first in six of seven events. But in 1976, the East Germans began making their move, winning three golds at Montreal. Since then, they have caught and passed the Soviets. The two countries each won four golds in the 1980 Olympics, and in the last two world championships the totals have been eighteen golds for the East Germans, fifteen for the Soviets. The rivalry will be more than two-sided at Lake Casitas, where Romania will also be represented by a strong team. The Romanian canoeists, led by Ivan Patzaichin and the much-improved Costica Olaru, won three golds in the 1983 world championships, which was a giant step up from their last Olympic showing (one gold, two silvers and two bronzes).

There will be twelve canoeing events in the L.A. Games, nine for the men and three for women, at Lake Casitas, which is part of a 6,200-acre recreation area in Ventura County, California, about eighty miles northwest of downtown Los Angeles. This is the first time since 1964 in Tokyo that a lake has been used for the Olympic canoeing competition. A

Top international canoeists turned up in September, 1983, to try out the new Olympic course at Lake Casitas near Ojai. Here, Sweden tops Italy in the 1,000-meter pairs kayak. AP Laserphoto

lake was most recently used in rowing at the 1960 Rome Games.

The Olympic events for men are kayak singles at 500 and 1,000 meters; kayak pairs at 500 and 1,000 meters; kayak fours at 1,000 meters; Canadian singles at 500 and 1,000 meters and Canadian pairs at 500 and 1,000 meters. The women's events are kayak singles at 500 meters; kayak pairs at 500 meters and kayak fours at 500 meters (a new event).

Kayakers sit in their boats, use a double-bladed paddle and stay on course with a foot-controlled rudder. Paddlers in the Canadian canoes kneel in the boats, use single-bladed paddles and control their direction with the paddle. The flatwater boats used in the Olympics are made of wood, a singles kayak being 17 feet long, 20 inches wide and weighing about 26 pounds. A one-person canoe is about 29 inches wide and weighs 35 pounds. Of all the canoes and kayaks, the kayak for the fours (K-4) is the fastest boat. A strong K-4 team would be capable of pulling a water skier. A typical K-4 is 36 feet long, 23½ inches wide and weighs 66 pounds.

Balance and strength are essential for a successful canoeist—never call them canoers, there is no such word—and teamwork is vital in the events for pairs and fours. Good starts are imperative and close finishes commonplace. At the end of the race, canoeists will shorten the length of their strokes while increasing the stroke rate. Water conditions have much to do with times. Patzaichin, for example, set the Olympic record of 4 minutes 8.94 seconds for the 1,000-meter Canadian singles in 1972; last year's winning time in the world championships was a slow 4:45.75, due to a strong wind factor.

Women's kayaking didn't become a part of the Olympics until 1948; kayaking pairs were introduced in 1960, and female fours will be seen for the first time at Lake Casitas. Only five countries have won gold medals in the women's events. The Soviets lead with eight, but the East Germans won both golds in 1980. Birgit Fischer of East Germany will try to win her second gold—she is a three-time world champion and is also a force in the pairs with teammate Carsta Kuhn. They won the world championships in 1981 and 1983.

In the women's events the U.S. has the best chance of winning a medal, but a high finish of any kind anywhere would be a surprise. American women have not won a medal in canoeing since 1964, and the last American gold medal by either sex in the sport came in 1952 at Helsinki, where Frank Havens finished first in the canoeing singles at the since-discontinued distance of 10,000 meters.

The best women's finisher in last year's world championships was Cathy Marino, a Long Beach, California, firefighter, who was sixth. "Kayaking is fun for me," Marino said. "My job can be a problem, because it drains you physically, and then you don't feel like giving one hundred percent to kayaking."

Rudy Helm has no such problems. "In my country," the West German said, "we have a lot of opportunities for young, talented athletes. I am financially independent because I am sponsored and I don't have to worry about work."

Helm's only worries this summer then are early to bed and early to rise. It will take at least an unscheduled series of morning waves at Lake Casitas to loosen his clutch on Olympic gold.

West German Ulrich Eicke outstrokes Tomas Buday of Hungary in the 1,000-meter Canadian singles. Eicke was eighth in the 500-meter event at Montreal in 1976. *AP Laserphoto*

ROWING

BY SEYMOUR BEUBIS

The Charles River in Boston, a few blocks from the hallowed halls of Harvard University, can be a brutal place in December, particularly when the wind howls and the thermometer is down around the 20-degree mark.

But there, in the early morning hours, looking from a distance like a speck in the water, is a 26-foot-long single scull manned by Christopher (Tiff) Wood, his fingers and face red and numb from the cold.

The 6-foot-1 185-pounder, who bears a resemblance to actor Tony Perkins, will battle the conditions for more than an hour on this day and every other until the river freezes around Christmas. Then, he will go indoors to continue his training on a rowing machine.

Such a regimen earned Wood a third-place finish in the single sculls event in the 1983 World Rowing Championships at Duisburg, West Germany, and he hopes it will also propel him to a berth on the U.S. Olympic rowing team in 1984.

Although he has been on two consecutive Olympic teams, Wood has yet to row a meter in the Games. He was an alternate in 1976 at Montreal and was to have captained the men's team at Moscow in 1980 while participating in the coxswainless quad sculls. But that was the year of the boycott.

"This is it for me," said Wood. "I could probably hang on for the Olympics in Korea in 1988, but, with the world situation, who knows if it will even take place? Besides, I want to get on with my life."

Considered the best bets to win medals for the U.S. in the competition at Lake Casitas are Wood and Virginia Gilder, twenty-five, also of Boston, who didn't compete until her freshman year at Yale but won a bronze medal in the single sculls in the world championships, and in the women's eight with coxswain, was a second-place finisher at the world championships.

Based on performance in the world championships, the chief competition for the American women will come from East Germany, the Soviet Union and Romania; for the men, Denmark, West Germany, East Germany, the Soviet Union, Great Britain, Spain, Norway and New Zealand.

Peter-Michael Kolbe of West Germany finished more than four seconds ahead of Wood in Duisburg (6:49.88 to 6:54.30), both very fast times. Gilder, 5-foot-7 and 145 pounds, has to contend with East Germany's Jutta Hampe, who

beat her by 3:36.51 to 3:39.05 at the world championships.

Wood, who works for a management consulting firm as a specialist in employee benefits, has been rowing for seventeen years and plans to continue for fun after the Olympics. "I do it because I love it," he said.

Gilder, who took up rowing "because it looked like it might be fun" and frequently works out on the Charles River with Wood and races against men once a week, has similar feelings for the sport.

"I have a life outside of rowing," she said. "I won't die if I don't win a medal, but I'd be lying if I said it wasn't very important."

Men's rowing races are all 2,000 meters long, women's events half that distance. The course is straight, six lanes wide, each lane of even depth. Six qualifiers in each event compete in the Olympic finals.

Competitive rowing has two categories: sweeps and sculls. In sweeps, each rower handles one long (12½ feet) oar. The three basic sweeps are pair, four and eight. Pairs and fours each have events with and without coxswain. Eights always have a coxswain, who sits in the stern, barks cadence and directs strategy and pace.

In sculls, each rower handles two oars approximately 10 feet long. The three sculling events are single, double and quadruple. The only sculling event with a coxswain is the women's quads.

The Olympics will have eight men's events: single, double and quadruple sculls; pairs with and without coxswain; fours with and without coxswain and eights with coxswain. The six women's events: single and double sculls; quadruple sculls with coxswain; pairs without coxswain and fours and eights with coxswain.

The U.S. Olympic teams will be selected from a combination of trials and all-star camps. There will be thirty men and twenty-four women. Coaches for the men are Harry Parker, coach at Harvard, sculls, and Kris Korzeniowski, former women's coach at Princeton, sweeps. Coaches for the women are Bob Ernst, women's coach at the University of Washington, sweeps, and John Van Blom of Long Beach, a four-time Olympic rower, sculls.

Most top rowers, particularly scullers, are from the Boston area or other eastern cities. There are also pockets of good rowers in Seattle, Long Beach, San Francisco and Madison, Wisconsin, at the University of Wisconsin.

Rowing is described by Wood as a "seven-minute endurance event. When you are finished, everything hurts. People think of it as a sport that is mostly

arms, but your legs and lungs hurt the most." Because of this, part of his training consists of running up hills and cross-country skiing, he said.

U.S. rowers have done well since the sport was included in the second of the modern Olympic Games—in Paris in 1900. That year, the American eight-man team from Vesper, a boat club in Philadelphia, was a gold medalist. In 1904 at St. Louis, American rowers won the gold in each of the five events offered. From 1920 through 1956, a crew from an American university took the gold medal in the eights each time.

But, as in other sports, the rest of the world has been catching up. At Melbourne in 1956, the Soviet Union won four medals, two of them gold, while the U.S. won six medals, three gold.

In 1976 at Montreal, the first time women's rowing was included in the Olympics, the East Germans became the super power, winning four golds in men's and four in women's while the U.S. managed but one silver medal in men's and a silver and bronze in women's.

Looking far too fragile to float eight burly oarsmen and a coxswain, the UCLA long boat warms up for a 1983 regatta. Photo by Rich Meyer/Los Angeles Times

Top left and right: *Christopher Wood of the U.S. won the single sculls in a pre-Olympic race on the Olympic rowing course at Lake Casitas.*

Above: *An East German pair surrenders to exhaustion at the end of a trial heat on Lake Casitas. Photos by Jose Galvez/Los Angeles Times*

YACHTING

BY RICH ROBERTS

Yacht racing was included when the Olympic Games were revived at Athens, Greece, in 1896, but apparently the gods did not approve. They blew up a storm that caused the competition to be canceled. There also were no races at St. Louis in 1904, officials reasoning that the Mississippi River is better for paddlewheelers than sailboats. But since then, the sport has grown to include seven classes of boats, each with entries from as many as forty nations, with one boat per class per country allowed.

You can't buy a ticket for yacht racing. There aren't any. And in recent Olympics going to see the races would have meant a long commute. In 1980, the yachting was 550 miles from Moscow at Tallin, Estonia; in 1976, a three-hour drive from Montreal at Kingston, Ontario, and in 1972 more than 600 miles from Munich at Kiel on the Baltic Sea. In 1984, however, it will be based at Long Beach, only about 25 miles from downtown Los Angeles, with races conducted on three triangular courses outside the east end of the Long Beach breakwater. Boardsailing, a new Olympic class, will take place inside the breakwater.

The 1984 Games will mark the first time since 1956 at Melbourne that the races will be contiguous with the main Olympic venue, but even that won't help the would-be spectators. For all of the viewing possibilities, the races might as well be on the Sea of Tranquility on the moon. The U.S. Coast Guard will keep spectator boats, official and private, well away from the courses in a tight, two-fold security program. They not only will tolerate no casual interference with the races, but are wary of terrorist actions. The best prospect for viewing may be closed-circuit television from helicopters beamed to yacht clubs in the area. It's a shame that, by its nature, the yachting must be conducted in such isolation that there will be no spectators to appreciate and applaud the competition, which is no less intense than the other sports played out before thousands.

Things were a little better in the 1932 Olympics, when the races were run several miles to the west off Cabrillo Beach outside Los Angeles Harbor. Spectators were able to follow the boats from the bluffs of Point Fermin and cheer the performances of skippers Owen Churchill and Gilbert Gray, who won America's first two gold medals in yachting. Churchill, now eighty-eight, is expected to attend the events aboard the restored 8-meter yacht *Angelita* he sailed fifty-two years ago.

The Long Beach site was selected for 1984 because of its more stable conditions—too stable, perhaps, for American sailors, who seem to do better in light and variable winds when crews must anticipate changes and adjust. The Long Beach courses were tested for suitability in three Olympic class events, starting in 1981. In 1983, when the winds blew hard and steady from the west, Americans suffered accordingly. That's why most of the top prospects agree that the 1984 yachting will be a "boat speed regatta," with the ability to read wind shifts a minor factor.

Ted Hinshaw, yachting commissioner for the Los Angeles Olympic Organizing Committee, said, "The most important thing is that the water off Long Beach is at its best at that time of year [July and August]. At Cabrillo, a lot of local knowledge is required because of the [nearby] land mass." Two other possibilities were Santa Monica Bay to the north and San Diego to the south, but the wind often is very light at those sites in the summer.

The rule of thumb in racing off Long Beach is to "go to the right." That means following the normal afternoon wind shift from southwest to west when beating to the windward mark. "Everything you read says that," says Dave Ullman, a three-time world champion in 470s class, who has spent most of his thirty-eight years sailing the same waters. "It happens not to be true. The area is very subtle. Local knowledge will be very, very important."

If that is true, American sailors may have an edge, after all. It didn't, however, show up in the 1983 Olympic Classes Regatta, but Ullman didn't compete then, either.

All of the classes are relatively small boats, unlike the 12-meter America's Cup sailing machines, and in the afternoon chop of San Pedro Bay they all become wet boats with no place to go to get dry. A two-hour race requires stamina, concentration and, in the classes with two- and three-man crews, teamwork.

The seven Olympic classes represent the four basic types of sailboats. The Solings and Stars have weighted keels for stability, while the 470s, Flying Dutchmans and Finns, with centerboards, rely totally on moving body weight around. The Tornado catamarans, twin hull boats, are the speedburners, capable of 30 knots in a blow. Sailboards, introduced for these Olympics, are the most basic of all—a sophisticated surfboard with a sail attached.

While sailboards were developed in the U.S., they have become even more popular in Europe. Boardsailing is America's weakest Olympic class. Stefan van den Berg of Holland is the favorite, but Scott Steele of Annapolis, Maryland, is given a chance to win a medal for the U.S.

Americans stand better in the other classes, particularly in Tornados, where world champion Randy Smyth of Huntington Beach, California, and crew Jay Glaser of Newport Beach have won every regatta they have entered over the last three years. An American also will be favored to win in Solings, the only boat with a three-man crew, although the competition will be keen among skippers Robbie Haines of San Diego, Dave Curtis of Marblehead, Massachusetts, and others to see who becomes the U.S. representative. A third U.S gold medal could come in the Star class where the veteran Bill Buchan of Bellevue, Washington, Vince Brun of San Diego or Peter Wright of Melrose Park, Illinois, are capable of beating the two-time world champion, Antonio Gorostegui of Spain.

Someone from New Zealand will be favored in the 470s—either David Barnes, the world champion in 1983, or Murray Jones, who has dominated the class since. Ullman, of Newport Beach, and Steve Benjamin of Oyster Bay, New York, give the U.S. an outside chance. Flying Dutchman is the least-defined class. Jonathon McKee of Kirkland, Washington, shocked everybody when he brought the U.S. its first world Flying Dutchman title in 1983, but that was in light, variable conditions in Sardinia, much different than what he'll have in Long Beach. The Europeans are generally stronger in Flying Dutchman, and the Soviet sailing team remains something of a mystery.

There will be seven races in each class, with each entry counting only his six best (one throwout). Reverse point scoring will be: from first through sixth, 0, 3, 5.7, 8, 10 and 11.7, and from seventh up, the place position plus 6. All protests will be reviewed by an international jury appointed by the International Yacht Racing Union, which will govern the event.

Dave Ullman is one of the U.S.'s leading amateur yachtsmen—and a successful professional sailmaker. Photo by Sam Mircovich/Los Angeles Times

Twin-hulled Tornado tests the westerly winds off Long Beach, where the Olympic yachting races will be contested. Photo by Ken Hively/Los Angeles Times

Above: *Hiking out to keep the boat in trim, a Flying Dutchman crewman and skipper test the waters off Los Angeles.*

Right: *More yachting classes have been dropped from Olympic competition than presently race in it, but Boardsailing— with equipment relatively inexpensive to transport and maintain—has been added. Photos by Ken Hively/Los Angeles Times*

SYNCHRONIZED SWIMMING

BY TRACY DODDS

When you see Tracie Ruiz and Candy Costie about to slide into an Olympic swiming pool, wearing synchronized rhinestone-studded Speedos, synchronized mascara, synchronized blusher, synchronized little flesh-colored noseplugs, synchronized topknots of hair made hard and fast by bobby pins and unflavored gelatin, synchronized caps and carefully synchronized smiles, it's easy to see why this sport has an identity crisis.

Certainly, the sport has come a long way since the days when beautiful women swam in glass tanks with fishes and eels, or the days when competitors floated in patterns wearing full Indian headdresses, Emmett Kelly costumes or Egyptian garb with rubber snakes coiled on the headpieces, but to deny the show business and aquacade background is to deny the ancestry that has had an obvious impact. It is also to deny the only image the public has of just what synchronized swimming is.

Synchronized swimming is making its debut as an Olympic sport in Los Angeles at the 1984 Summer Games. Then and there the world will see why synchronized swimming is—and is not—the same art form brought to life by Esther Williams in a series of MGM films in the 1940s and 1950s. Esther Williams, who has been honored as the First Lady of synchronized swimming, epitomizes the ongoing identity crisis within the sport, a crisis between the theatrical image and the athletic excellence needed to perform well. Williams, of course, was the national freestyle champion before she became famous for her glamorous Hollywood routines. But she was a pioneer in aquatic art, an art that has evolved through several eras since the turn of the century. As it is now, there is still theatrical influence, just as in figure skating and gymnastics, where music, choreography and costuming are utilized. Synchronized swimmers are seeking the same respect as athletes that is already afforded to skaters and gymnasts.

To be a synchronized swimmer requires the endurance of a speed swimmer, the coordination of a gymnast and the grace of a dancer.

Ruiz and Costie, the duet favored to represent the U.S. in the Games, work in jazz, ballet, weight training and running, besides swimming every day. They have the ability to swim the length of the pool underwater, propel themselves above the surface like Polaris missiles, do turns and spins and seemingly impossible maneuvers, smiling and making it look effortless all the while.

It's a wonderful sport for spectators, and for television, which is why synchronized swimming officials feel so confident that the Olympic exposure will escalate interest in the sport. Synchronized swimming was one of the earliest sellouts in the 1984 Games. Synchro crowds have been surpassing swimming crowds at the last several international competitions, even though the sport is in its fledgling stages.

In the Olympics there will be competition in just one of three categories, the duet competition. There will be no solo competition, no teams of eight. Actually, the team routines have a greater spectator appeal, but Olympic organizers wanted to keep the numbers of competitors down and decided that instead of limiting the number of countries that could qualify to enter a team, it would be better to see how many countries would be interested in entering a duet. Some countries won't enter simply because the U.S. dominance is so strong. There is beginning to be a parity among the thirty or more countries involved in synchronized swimming, but, historically, the Americans have stolen the show. This is, after all, a sport born and raised in the Hollywood image.

Those who have sought a historical perspective report that the Assyrian palace of Nimrod had underwater swimmers as far back as 880 B.C. There are also ancient Japanese woodblock prints showing male swimmers performing somersaults and ballet-leg stunts. The first modern-day swimmer to gain acclaim for aquatic art was Annette Kellerman, a fifteen-year-old Australian who did what she called "ornamental swimming" in 1907 in an aquatic show in Melbourne. Her partners in the tank were fishes and eels. Kellerman made two films, including *Daughters of the Gods*.

Synchronized swimming was developed as a competitive sport by Katherine Curtis, an instructor at the University of Wisconsin in 1916. She continued to develop the sport at the University of Chicago. At the Chicago World's Fair in 1934, Curtis's unique form of artistic sport gained attention. The "Kay Curtis Modern Mermaids" performed three shows a day throughout the World's Fair. The mermaids were a hit, so others got into the act. Billy Rose presented the Aquacade at the 1939 World's Fair in San Francisco. One of the stars of that show was Esther Williams.

Also in San Francisco, the Fairmont Hotel held annual Water Follies. Dawn Bean, who is now competition director for synchronized swimming at the 1984 Olympics, swam in the Fairmont show. She later became an American and Pan Am Games champion.

Interest spread to Europe when Beulah Gundling, the first national outdoor champion, made tours abroad in the 1940s, giving demonstrations. The sport got its biggest boost internationally when it was included in the Pan Am Games in 1955. The Pan Am Games dropped the sport in 1959, brought it back in 1963, dropped it again in 1967 and brought it back in 1971.

Curtis wrote the original textbook on the sport and set up the method of scoring, which has undergone some evolution. Rules were based on competitive diving. Different moves are designated to have varying degrees of difficulty and competitors are judged according to the perfection of their execution. By the time the four-minute duet routines are performed before sellout crowds in Los Angeles, each swimmer wil have gone through a series of six compulsory figures for the judges. The duet routines themselves are later judged for their overall effectiveness.

Traditionally, twins have had much success with duet competition. Karen and Sarah Josephson of Ohio State are one of the top teams in the United States now. But Ruiz and Costie, both twenty and both from Seattle, have been dominating national competition leading to the Olympics and also doing well internationally. They have been working together since they were ten and now they are closing in on a gold medal. At the world championships in Guayaquil in 1982 (where tickets were being scalped at two and three times their face value), Ruiz won the solo title and the Canadian team of Kelly Kryczka and Sharon Hambrook won the duet title.

At the Pan Am Games in Caracas last summer, Ruiz and Costie won the duet title. Penny and Vicky Vilagos, twins from Canada, finished second, and Canada won the team title. In 1983, Ruiz and Costie also won the U.S. senior nationals for the third straight year and the American Cup, held in the Olympic pool in Los Angeles. Ruiz and Costie should get strong competition from Canada and Japan. Great Britain, Switzerland, West Germany, France, Holland, Mexico and Cuba have been closing the gap lately in this new event, which, for many, will bring back old memories.

Getting used to gold, America's top duet synchronized swimmers Candy Costie and Tracie Ruiz give high fives to the crowd at a Los Angeles meet in 1983. Photo by Con Keyes/Los Angeles Times

Canada fields a strong pair in the duet synchronized swim in Sharon Hambrook and Kelly Kryczka. Photo by Con Keyes/Los Angeles Times

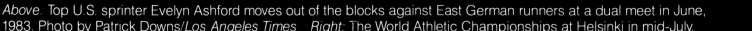

Above: Top U.S. sprinter Evelyn Ashford moves out of the blocks against East German runners at a dual meet in June, 1983. Photo by Patrick Downs/*Los Angeles Times. Right:* The World Athletic Championships at Helsinki in mid-July,

1983, presaged many likely match-ups for 1984. Here, U.S.A.'s Carl Lewis takes the baton from Calvin Smith in a world-record 4 x 100-meter relay. Photo by Juha Jormanainen/Woodfin Camp

Cuban 800-meter specialist Alberto Juantorena, the 1976 gold-medalist, goes out front. Photo by Patrick Downs/
Los Angeles Times

Top: U.S. middle distance runner Rosalyn Bryant. *Above:* Top American hurdler Edwin Moses. Photos by Patrick Downs/*Los Angeles Times*

Above and opposite: World-class 1,500-meter specialists: Mary Decker; Steve Scott, in front, with Tom Byers, at rear, closing fast. Photos by Patrick Downs/*Los Angeles Times*

Above left: East German shot-putter Udo Beyer holds the world's record. *Above right:* Hammer thrower Ed Burke gives it

a heave. Photos by Patrick Downs/*Los Angeles Times*

Above left: British decathlon star Daley Thompson heaves the javelin.　*Above right:* Martina Opitz of East Germany took

world discus honors at Helsinki. Photos by Juha Jormanainen/Woodfin Camp

Inset: Rhythmic gymnastics—with ball, hoop, clubs and ribbon—is new for the 1984 Olympics. Photo by Kishimoto Corp. Julianne McNamara, U.S.A., on the balance beam. Photo by Tony Barnard/*Los Angeles Times*

Above: Uneven parallel bars offer women gymnasts their most spectacular event. Photo by Gary Friedman/*Los Angeles Times.* *Inset:* Kathy Johnson shows excellent form. Photo by Tony Barnard/*Los Angeles Times.*

First-rate U.S. gymnasts: Peter Vidmar (*left*) on the rings; Matt Arnot (*right*) on the parallel bars.
Photos by Tony Barnard/*Los Angeles Times*

Mario McCutcheon on the horizontal bar. Photo by Tony Barnard/*Los Angeles Times*

UCLA's Mitch Gaylord swings through a change on the pommel horse. Photo by Gary Friedman/*Los Angeles Times*

GYMNASTICS

BY RICHARD HOFFER

Until 1972, our national awareness of the game was such that reports of a Tsukahara vault were more likely directed to bankers than to gymnasts. Here, gymnastics was regarded as a kind of compulsive aerobics, a cult activity that was fun enough to watch, in a casual way, but way too hard to do. Until 1972, the U.S. was about as forward in this sport as a backward somersault. The country that could put a man on the moon couldn't get an eighty-pound girl off the balance beam without some kind of international misadventure.

But then came 1972, the year of Olga, when white-ribboned pigtails became every girl's favorite fashion accessory and gymnastics became everybody's glamour event. Gymnastics, of course, had already been around a long time by the Munich Olympics and was highly popular in other parts of the world. But until worldwide television brought into our living rooms the Soviet Union's Olga Korbut, an eighty-four-pound sprite whose smiles and tears earned her a place in our hearts, few here had any idea what a spectacle this was.

There were two aspects to Olga's considerable influence on the sport, one that actually altered its course and another that helped push the U.S. into it in a big way. Number One was the introduction of a bold and daring style, a recklessness on the apparatus that startled—even scared—other accomplished gymnasts and coaches. Up to then, women's gymnastics had been dominated by graceful ballerinas, dancers who emphasized a purity and artistry of motion. And then came Olga with her back somersaults off the beam and uneven bars, movements actually considered ugly to the purists at the time, but considered spectacular to everyone else.

As we move into the 1984 Olympics, twelve years later, it is difficult to remember how amazing Olga Korbut's routines were and what frontiers they expanded. Believe it or not, there was some outrage at the time, as if the ballet had been given over to high-wire artists. Some judges even wanted to ban some of her moves. But most others who saw Olga knew immediately that the sport would henceforth be in the hands of brave little acrobats, athletes who as yet had not been introduced to the gloomy effects of gravity.

Number Two, and certainly more important to the ensuing popularity of the sport in the U.S., was Olga's show-manship. Don Peters, now the U.S. women's Olympic coach, remembers Olga less for her routines than for her behavior, bizarre by gymnastics standards of the day. "When she walked into the arena," he recalls, "she waved." It is Peters's feeling that the gymnastics world, which liked a stoic and suffering face on its players, couldn't have been more shocked if Olga had done her parade lap on a Harley Davidson. As if that toothy grin didn't have enough impact, Olga showed yet another face. After a disastrous routine, which denied her some medals, she broke down in tears, crying into her cupped hands. That did it. Thereafter, every little girl acrobat wanted to be just like Olga. And the sport rocketed.

After Olga demonstrated the sport's popularity that year, and again in 1976, after Romania's Nadia Comaneci, a steely perfectionist, upped the ante in bravery on bars, a lot of preteens went into seclusion in gymnastics clubs throughout this country, suddenly preferring tumbling to ballroom dance. What an impact these two girls had. You can't talk to an experienced gymnast today without hearing Olga's or Nadia's name invoked. Within a decade in the U.S., a pool of some 15,000 women gymnasts would grow to 150,000. Some of the clubs were good and some of the gymnasts were, too. The momentum was secured and the U.S. was on its way.

(The American boycott of the Olympics in 1980 may have stalled that momentum some; without another gymnastics heroine and another impetus for the preteens to choose gymnastics over other activities once more, the sport's popularity has waned a little according to club owners, suggesting that the next generation of gymnasts here will be from a smaller pool of talent.)

Worldwide, though, Olga's impact was different, though no less powerful. In fact, as you watch the gymnastics competition this year, you will be enjoying Olga's legacy, more than any other gymnast's. Not that she was such a great gymnast; a last-minute replacement, she wasn't even on the Soviet Union's roster for those games and her performances thereafter were inconsistent enough to cause some revisionist thinking concerning her ability. No, it's not the tricks and routines that she left us, but rather her style, a high-flying and adventuresome style, a style that lent itself to innovative daredevils.

Today's gymnastics, both for men and women, is such a fast-changing sport, thanks to Olga, that even the top participants are hard-pressed to keep up with it. New, "impossible" routines are being perfected daily. A competition doesn't go by that something revolutionary isn't unveiled.

Innovation is the key word in gymnastics and has been for some time. Pity the poor gymnast who spends long hours in the gym perfecting a routine that dazzled everybody in the last competition. She would be properly mortified by the advances made since then. In this sport, where some countries (read: USSR) employ scientists just to think up possible new movements as many as six years before the trick will be introduced, he who stands pat stands alone, and not on the awards podium, either.

How fast is this sport moving? Well, at the world championships in Budapest last year, even the judges were a little confused by what they saw. Everything looked good to them; discrimination amidst all this excellence was no longer possible, and they awarded no fewer than thirty-three perfect scores. "They are doing movements of such originality, risk and perfection," said a gymnastics official, "that they can't help but score 10s."

Aside from Olga, and the heated imperatives the East European countries place on international competition, there have been developments within the sport to accelerate its advancement. The equipment has been improved, for one thing. Once gymnasts did their floor exercises on a wooden gymnasium floor, not very conducive to hard tumbling. Now, they perform double, twisting somersaults across a spring-loaded platform, getting added thrusts for takeoffs (and softer splashdowns) from the equipment. And, too, the athletes have improved, both by virtue of more sophisticated training facilities and coaching and a kind of evolution. The men's competition has always rewarded strength, so muscles have long been in evidence. But the bodies of women gymnasts have changed markedly since the sport has taken its acrobatic turn. Now they are younger, shorter and lighter—more compact—yet still stronger, the better to accomplish the powerful tumbling that is now in vogue.

This is all to say that gymnastics is becoming different and better and more exciting. Once, the sport was meant to celebrate poise and posture, balance and strength. Today it gives us dangerous and continuous movement. An event like the parallel bars was first meant to show how well a man could maintain his balance; today if a competitor pauses more than three times on the apparatus, points are deducted. Nobody pauses. And an event like the balance beam was at first meant to demonstrate a woman's balletic balance, as if just to walk the length of a four-inch slab of wood was worthy of a medal. Today, several aerials are required to earn really high scores. And who knows where it's headed.

Far easier to say where it's come from. When it was first introduced as an Olympic sport back in 1898, men's gymnastics was a weird competition, a sort of athletic "Gong Show," including such events as club swinging, rope climbing and the heaving of a 110-pound weight. By 1924, the competition was pared down to the six events contested today—the rings, the pommel horse, the vault, the parallel bars, the horizontal bar and the floor exercise. Women joined the competition four years later and by 1952 settled on the uneven bars, the vault, the beam and the floor exercise.

In the years since then, the Eastern European countries have maintained a dominance that has not been often interrupted. The Soviet women, who are once more favored come Olympic time in Los Angeles, have been ruling this sport roughly forever. And they look strong again. There have been reports that their world championship team will be almost entirely overhauled by this summer, a touch of overkill as far as the competition is concerned. Only the Romanians, who have retooled since the retirement of Nadia and the defection of coaches Bela and Marta Karolyi to the U.S., stand to challenge them.

The men's competition, on the other hand, could be a little less predictable. The Soviet men, who have won all but five team titles since they joined the Olympics (the Japanese were the only team to interrupt their reign), were upset by China in last year's world championships. They weren't beaten by much and they did manage to win most of the other medals in the competition. Still, China, with its emphasis on powerful tumbling, suddenly looms as a power. An interesting battle for individual titles shapes up between sixteen-year-old Dmitri Belozerchev, the new Soviet king, and China's Lee Ning.

Neither the U.S. women nor the U.S. men will be challenging for anything higher than third in the team standings and, privately, many of the sport's top organizers concede that would be reaching. National commitment to this sport will never be the same here as in Eastern Europe, where athletic excellence is used as a political tool. Here, the sport is run with an entrepreneurial spirit, with individual coaches and clubs competing for the top athletes and the top places. The sport is expensive, with a year's training for an elite woman gymnast pegged at eight to fifteen thousand dollars. And there is scarcely any national funding for it. As for the men, it is probably just as expensive, although the NCAA ends up footing the bill for their collegiate training.

All the same, because of its recent popularity here, U.S. gymnastics has become highly competitive worldwide. Whereas once it was possible for somebody like Muriel Grossfeld, a three-time Olympian, to just take up the sport and actually make an Olympic team with three weeks of training, the U.S. has now advanced to the forefront; only gymnasts with upward of ten years experience need apply. But if the U.S. does get shut out of a team medal, there are others possible. For there are more than just team competitions in gymnastics. An Olympic meet is actually three competitions in one. The team competition takes up two days of gymnastics, one for compulsory routines and one for optionals. The individual all-around is contested by the top thirty-six scorers from the team competition (but no more than three from any one team); the contenders compete in optional exercises a third day and their scores here are added to their scores from the team competition. Finally, the top six in each event (with no more than two from a team) compete for the individual event medals.

With these many competitions, a male gymnast can collect a possible eight medals. That may seem inflationary, but consider the number of unrelated skills he must master. Only in the decathlon must an athlete master as many events as the gymnast. There can be no specialists here; the premium is on all-around excellence.

Part of the fun of watching gymnastics, depending on your point of view, is seeing how this excellence is judged. There are some absolutes in the judging—falling off a beam is a .5 deduction, stepping out of bounds during floor exercises is a .1 deduction. Yet much of it is highly subjective. Often this subjectivity is linked to the judge's political background, raising an occasional furor over bias and favoritism. Most agree that the right person usually wins the meet. Yet experts also agree that a lot of medal juggling is performed beyond the actual apparatus.

At this Olympics, with Los Angeles as the home court, some coaches and officials expect a softening of the East European bias. Along with that, they're hoping for a payoff in performance that little Olga prompted more than a decade ago.

Valentin Pinter of Romania takes first place in the floor exercise. Photo by Gary Friedman/Los Angeles Times

Above: *Jean Choquette of Canada on the parallel bars.*
Left: *Mitsuoki Watanabe of Japan does a one-arm giant swing on the horizontal bar.*
Photos by Gary Friedman/
Los Angeles Times

Top: *U.S.A.'s Peter Vidmar in the floor exercise. Photo by Gary Friedman/ Los Angeles Times*

Above: *Mary Lou Retton of the U.S. took four individual firsts at a meet in Las Vegas in February 1984. Photo by Tony Barnard/Los Angeles Times*

Left: *Yvonne Haug of France in the floor exercise. Photo by Gary Friedman/ Los Angeles Times*

Top left: *Mitsuoki Watanabe of Japan on the pommel horse. Photo by Gary Friedman/Los Angeles Times*

Top right: *Julianne McNamara has been a mainstay of the U.S. women's gymnastics team, which hopes to do better than it did in the world championships last year. The team finished seventh. Photo by Tony Barnard/Los Angeles Times*

Above: *A demonstration of acrobatic movement with apparatus—called rhythmic gymnastics. Photo by Gary Friedman/Los Angeles Times*

SPRINTS AND HURDLES

BY MAL FLORENCE

Although the United States, with sixty medals, has traditionally dominated the sprints in the Olympic Games, it hasn't won a gold medal in the 100 or 200 meters since 1968. But it seems safe to say that American sprinters will be back on the gold standard in the 1984 Olympics in Los Angeles.

The men's sprint corps is possibly the strongest since the advent of the modern Olympics in 1896. This was underscored in the World Track Championships last August in Helsinki, when the U.S. swept the 100 and won gold and silver medals in the 200. And the Americans could have swept the 200 had Carl Lewis not passed up the race to concentrate on the 100, long jump and his anchor leg of the 400-meter relay team. He won the 100 and long jump and brought the 400 team home with a gold medal in a world record time of 37.86 seconds. So it is conceivable that the U.S. could sweep the 100 and 200 to become the first country to accomplish such a feat since the Americans did it in the 1904 Olympics in St. Louis. If not, the U.S. will be heavily favored to get gold and silver medals in each sprint.

Lewis and Calvin Smith have proven that they are in a class of their own in the sprints. Lewis not only won the 100 at Helsinki but was a double sprint winner in The Athletics Congress meet last year. His 200 time of 19.75 is the fastest ever at sea level. Smith is the world record-holder in the 100 at 9.93—a time recorded last July at high altitude in Colorado Springs. Smith also won the Helsinki 200 and, significantly, then beat Lewis in both sprints a few weeks later at Zurich, Switzerland. It was a historic one-day double as Smith was timed at 9.97 in the 100—equaling Lewis's fastest ever time at sea level—and came back with a 19.99 in the 200.

Beyond Lewis and Smith, U.S. hopefuls are Emmit King, who finished third in the Helsinki 100; Elliot Quow, a surprise silver medalist in the 200; Larry Myricks, Ron Brown, Jeff Phillips, Mel Lattany and, possibly, James Sanford, a top-ranked sprinter in 1979, who is making a comeback from a chronic foot injury. Myricks, who has a best 200 time of 20.03, hadn't sufficiently recovered from a hamstring injury and was eliminated in a first-round heat at Helsinki. Brown, who beat Lewis in one 100 in 1983, didn't qualify for the U.S. team at Helsinki because of a minor leg injury.

Obviously serious about his medal pursuit, he passed up a three-year, $900,000 pro football contract with the Cleveland Browns in order to compete in the Olympics.

Based on the results at Helsinki, foreign sprinters seem incapable of challenging the Americans for gold and silver medals. One with a chance is Britain's Allan Wells, the 1980 Olympic 100 winner at Moscow, who finished fourth at Helsinki. He wasn't in the best of shape, however, and could break up an American sweep in Los Angeles. Italy's Pietro Mennea is another with an outside chance. If he makes the 200 final in Los Angeles, he will become the only athlete to be a sprint finalist in four Olympics. The best Mennea, thirty-two, could do at Helsinki was third behind Smith and Quow.

"Any sprinter who makes the U.S. team has a chance to win a gold medal in the Olympics," said Lewis, who is expected to compete in four events at Los Angeles—100, 200, long jump and sprint relay.

In the 400 meters, considered a sprint by track experts, form took a beating at Helsinki. Michael Franks and Sunder Nix of the U.S. made surprise showings, winning silver and bronze medals behind Jamaica's Bert Cameron. Cameron is the best quarter-miler in the world and was favored to win. But Hartmut Weber of West Germany, the European champion, was recovering from a virus and finished fifth, one place behind countryman Erwin Skamrahl, who later had a 1983 world's best time of 44.50. Cameron won at Helsinki in 45.02. Viktor Martin of the Soviet Union, the 1980 Olympic gold medal winner, didn't even make the final. Thomas Schonlebe, who beat Americans Eliot Tabron and Franks in the U.S.-East Germany dual meet in June of 1983, was sixth. The only other Americans who might figure in the L.A. 400 are veterans Cliff Wiley and Walter McCoy and a schoolboy star from Pittsburgh named Clinton Davis.

If anyone qualifies as a cinch medalist in the 1984 Games, it would be the incomparable Edwin Moses in the 400-meter intermediate hurdles. Moses came back in 1983 from a year's layoff to reassert his dominance in the event. Not only did he win at Helsinki, but he later lowered his world record to 47.02 seconds. The 1976 Montreal Olympic champion is now unbeaten in eighty-seven finals. (The last he lost was in 1977.) The real race is expected to be the one behind Moses. Harald Schmid of West Germany, runner-up to Moses at Helsinki, figures to win a medal at Los Angeles. Other possibilities are Andre Phillips of the U.S., who became the

third-fastest performer ever in 1983 with a time of 47.78; Alexander Kharlov of the Soviet Union, who was third at Helsinki; Sven Nylander of Sweden; David Lee of the U.S.; and Volker Beck of East Germany, the 1980 Moscow winner, who has been hampered by injuries.

In the 110-meter hurdles, Greg Foster of the U.S. is clearly the best in the world. He no longer runs in the shadow of Renaldo Nehemiah, the world record-holder (12.93), who is now a wide receiver with pro football's San Francisco 49ers. Nehemiah's pro status makes him ineligible for Olympic competition. The powerful Foster (6-foot-3, 190 pounds), who sometimes crashes into hurdles as he did in Helsinki, where he barely won, is not the almost certain winner that Moses is. The U.S. lost yet another medal prospect in the 110 hurdles to football when Willie Gault signed a contract with the Chicago Bears. That left Arto Brygarre of Finland, runner-up to Foster at Helsinki; Thomas Munkelt of East Germany, the 1980 Moscow Olympic champion; Sam Turner and Tonie Campbell of the U.S.; Mark McCoy of Canada; and Gyorgy Bakos of Hungary.

The women's sprints should provide considerable drama, especially the 100 meters, where Marlies Gohr of East Germany and Evelyn Ashford of the U.S. resume their rivalry. Ashford, the world 100 record-holder at 10.79 seconds, had beaten Gohr in four of five meetings until the U.S.-East Germany dual meet. Gohr won that one and then beat Ashford in Helsinki when the American sprinter collapsed on the track in the final with a pulled hamstring muscle in her right leg. Ashford has had ample time to recover from her injury and challenge Gohr. But if she doesn't get the gold medal in the 100, she might get it in the 200. Marita Koch of East Germany, the world record-holder in the race, probably will compete only in the 400 because event scheduling in the Olympics makes it difficult to qualify in both the 200 and 400. Jarmila Kratochvilova, the wonder woman from Czechoslovakia, will not compete in both the 400 and 800 in Los Angeles. The Olympic schedule precludes a double for her. She won both races in Helsinki, setting a world record of 47.99 in the 400.

Other women sprinters/quarter-milers who are medal prospects in the Olympics include Diane Williams of the U.S. (100), Merlene Ottey of Jamaica (100 and 200), Angela Bailey of Canada (100), Florence Griffith of the U.S. (200), Kathy Cook of Great Britain (200), Tatiana Kocembova of Czechoslovakia and Maria Pingina of the Soviet Union

(400). The women's hurdles most likely will be dominated by athletes from Eastern European countries. Bettine Jahn and Kerstin Knabe, who finished 1-2 in the 100-meter hurdles at Helsinki, are the best in the world. The same can be said of the gold, silver and bronze medalists in the 400 hurdles at Helsinki—Yekaterina Fesenko and Anna Ambrosene of the Soviet Union and Ellen Fiedler of East Germany. Americans Benita Fitzgerald and Candy Young are medalist longshots.

Below left: *Edwin Moses of the U.S. came into 1984 with an 87-meet winning streak in 400-meter hurdles. Photo by Joe Kennedy/Los Angeles Times*

Below right: *Marlies Gohr (near lane) of East Germany hits the finish line with a convincing victory in the 100-meter dash at the world championships in Helsinki, Finland. Gohr's biggest rival is Evelyn Ashford of the U.S. Photo by Woodfin Camp Assoc.*

Bottom: *U.S.A.'s Greg Foster easily wins the 110-meter hurdles in a dual meet with East Germany. Foster won at Helsinki and has often more than bettered medal-winning times of the 1980 Games. Photo by Patrick Downs/Los Angeles Times*

Carl Lewis (second from right) is behind the leaders at this stage of the 100-meter dash final at the world championships, but he didn't stay there. Lewis's great acceleration carried him to one of his three victories at Helsinki. His time: 10.07 seconds. Photo by Woodfin Camp Assoc.

MIDDLE AND LONG DISTANCES

BY BILL SHIRLEY

Historically, the longer the footrace, the harder it has been for an American to win an Olympic medal. At Los Angeles in 1984, the American men are unlikely to win more than one race longer than 400 meters, and they'll probably be upstaged by a fragile little American woman. Mary Decker not only is expected to win a medal in both the 1,500 and 3,000 meters, she has a good shot at a gold in the 3,000.

Two American men, Henry Marsh in the 3,000-meter steeplechase and Steve Scott in the 1,500 meters, will be strong contenders for medals, but only Marsh appears to have a chance to win his race. Doug Padilla is a longer shot for a medal in the 5,000. And that just about sums up the United States's hopes in the middle- and long-distance races. Soviet Union men probably will fare as poorly as U.S. males. No Soviet man ran fast enough to make the *Track and Field News*'s 1983 list of top twenty performers in distances from 800 through 10,000 meters.

Oddly, only in the shortest of the middle-distance races, the 800 meters, has the U.S. had much success in the Olympics, winning the event eight times since it was first run in 1896. U.S. men have won the 1,500 meters, the glamour event of track and field, only twice, the last time in 1908. In 1952, Horace Ashenfelter became the only American winner of the steeplechase. In 1964, Bob Schul and Billy Mills won the 5,000 and 10,000 meters, races no other Americans have ever won.

Here's how the men's races shape up for the Olympics:

1,500—The favorites are all named Steve. Last names: Cram, Ovett, Scott. England's Ovett, the 1980 Olympic 800 champion, holds the world record at 3:30.17. But Cram, twenty-two, is rapidly developing into Great Britain's best runner. No. 1 in the world in 1982, he ran the 1,500 in 3:31.66 in 1983 and also ran the fastest 800 of the year, 1:43.61. He won the world championship at Helsinki in a tactical race in 3:41.59, with Scott second and Ovett fourth. Absent at Helsinki—and from many other races last year—was England's Sebastian Coe, the 1980 Olympic champion at 1,500 meters, who was unable to run for three months due to a glandular ailment. His best time in 1983 was 3:35.17. A healthy Coe would be favored to win a gold medal in either the 800 or 1,500. Sydney Maree,

a South African who applied for U.S. citizenship, has run a 3:31.24—a world record for a week last summer before Ovett reclaimed it—but is noted as much for his inconsistency as his speed. Ovett set the record in a blustery wind last September and said, "Under ideal conditions, I can break 3:30." The conditions at Los Angeles's Coliseum probably will be ideal, but the Olympic 1,500, as well as other races, is likely to be more a tactical race than a run for a record. To most runners, an Olympic gold medal is more important.

800—There was unprecedented depth in 1983, with eighteen runners under 1:45, led by Cram and Willi Wulbeck of West Germany, who won the world championship in 1:43.65. Wulbeck, Rob Druppers of Holland and Joaquim Cruz of Brazil are likely to be strong candidates for medals; Cram is, too, unless he runs only the 1,500. Druppers was second and Cruz third at Helsinki. James Robinson, Don Paige, David Mack and David Patrick were the best the U.S. had in 1983 but lack the others' speed. Cuba's Alberto Juantorena broke a foot at Helsinki but said he expects to run in the Olympics.

5,000—Eamonn Coghlan of Ireland won the biggest race of 1983, the world championship, but Portugal's Fernando Mamede had the two fastest times and three of the fastest five. His best was 13:08.54. Coghlan virtually jogged to victory at Helsinki in 13:28.53, beating Werner Schildhauer of East Germany and Martti Vainio of Finland. However, he had only the twenty-third best time in the world in 1983 at 13:23.53. David Moorcroft of England, the world record-holder at 13:00.42, missed most of 1983 with an injury but is expected to compete at Los Angeles. Other contenders are Padilla, whose 1983 best was 13:17.69, Antonio Leitao of Portugal and Hansjorg Kunze of East Germany.

10,000—Schildhauer, Kunze, Vainio and Mamede are among the best in this race, too, along with Portugal's Carlos Lopes and Italy's Alberto Cova. Lopes had the fastest 1983 time of 27:23.44, but Cova won the world title, beating Schildhauer and Kunze in 28:01.04. Lopes finished sixth. Mamede, a fast qualifier, has not run well in major championships.

Steeplechase—Marsh, the American record-holder at 8:12.37, the fastest time in the world in 1983, hit the last hurdle and finished eighth at Helsinki. The race was won in 8:15.05 by Patriz Ilg of West Germany, who had two of the fastest times in the world in 1983 and probably will be favored. But Marsh could win it. Other contenders besides Marsh are Boguslaw Maminski of Poland, Colin Reitz of Great Britain, Joseph Mahmoud

of France and Graeme Fell of Great Britain.

The women's races:

Decker, overcoming her fragility, a broken marriage and the Soviets, was perhaps the best female runner in the world in 1983 in the 1,500 and 3,000. Free of injuries, she ran three of the four fastest 1,500s—including the fastest at 3:57.12, an American record—three of the ten fastest 3,000s and won both races at Helsinki. However, she will have a flock of swift Soviet runners to beat at Los Angeles, including world record-holders Tatyana Kazankina (3:52.47 in the 1,500) and Svyetlana Ulmasova (8:26.78 in the 3,000). At her best, Decker would be pressed to match those times, but she beat both Kazankina and Ulmasova at Helsinki. West Germany's Brigitte Kraus is a strong threat in the 3,000. Jarmila Kratochvilova of Czechoslovakia appears unbeatable in the 800. She set the world record at 1:53.28 and says she is still learning how to run the race. If she doesn't fall down, everyone else will run for second place at Los Angeles. Kratochvilova also holds the world record in the 400, but it will be virtually impossible for her to run both races in the Olympics because of the schedule. At Helsinki she said, "I think I'll concentrate on one event.... I think it might be the 800."

Kratochvilova's time in the 800 would have astonished the world in 1928, the first year women were allowed to compete in track and field in the Olympics. The 800 time then was 2:16.80 and, one historian reported, "There was much unfavorable comment after the 800 meters, owing to the apparent distress of some of the contestants."

No women's races in 1932 were longer than 100 meters. They ran 200 meters in 1948, the 800 was restored in 1960 and the 1,500 was run for the first time in 1972. The 3,000 will be a new event at Los Angeles.

For years, Mary Decker has been
America's best from 1,500 to 10,000
meters, but she was suspect on the
international circuit. No more. Decker
showed her competitive fire with
a great double victory at the world
championships last year, including this
one at 1,500 meters. That's Zamira
Zaytseva of the Soviet Union taking a spill.
Photo by Woodfin Camp Assoc.

A jubilant Eamonn Coghlan of Eire wins
the 5,000-meters at Helsinki, although
slow at 13:28.53. A highly successful
indoor miler, Coghlan was fourth in the
5,000 at Moscow. Photo by Woodfin
Camp Assoc.

One of the more grueling Olympic events is the 3,000-meter steeplechase, when men make like horses negotiating twenty-eight hurdles and seven water jumps. Above, U.S. and East German runners try out the Coliseum track. Photo by Patrick Downs/Los Angeles Times

Willi Wulbeck of West Germany, fourth in the 1976 Olympics, won the 800 meters at Helsinki when Alberto Juantorena, the great Cuban, scratched. Photo by Woodfin Camp Assoc.

MEN'S MARATHON

BY RICK REILLY

It is the reflection of Cierpinski's steps on the rainy streets of Montreal, the stunned face of Shorter in Munich. It is the relentlessness of Zatopek in Helsinki, the grim countenance of Mamo Wolde in Mexico City. It is 26 miles 385 yards of calculated insanity, the Olympics' no-frills event. No judges. No teammates. No breaks. Just grown men seeing who wants to push blood and bone and sinew the farthest.

It is the culmination of the Olympics, its definitive event, its oldest show. It has put wreaths around the heads of a Czech legend (Emil Zatopek, 1952, Helsinki), an Ethiopian Army sergeant (Wolde, 1968, Mexico City), an Argentine newspaper carrier (Juan Zabala, 1932, Los Angeles) and a French car mechanic (Alain Mimoun, 1956, Melbourne).

It is the Olympic marathon, rich in guts and glitter, so much so that when it is over, the Olympics are over. The finish of the 1984 men's marathon in L.A. will signal the beginning of the closing ceremonies. And that is how it should be— as if to say that one more event would be anticlimactic.

It is Sunday, August 12, 1984, and ABC-TV knows there are tingles to be gleaned from that day. That is why they will televise the marathon live. Television loves shots of men nearing exhaustion—clomping and churning as they go—expressionless. But with a starting time of 5:30 P.M. in the belly of a Los Angeles August?

"Nobody runs a marathon in Los Angeles in August," says nationally known running writer Joe Henderson. Henderson was one of many who had asked for a less sadistic start, either early morning or dusk. But the Olympic people said no. Five-thirty is the cool, cool, cool of the evening, they said. An afternoon jog along the Pacific Ocean and then a tour through scenic West L.A. will be delightful, they said. But not to run 26-plus miles. For it is neither cool nor evening. The average high temperature for that date in Los Angeles is 84 degrees. Groan. So great is the potential for smog and heat that the Olympic equestrian events were moved out of Los Angeles so the horses wouldn't have to breathe the stuff.

"A ghastly thing" is how New York City Marathon Director Fred Lebow describes it. But never mind him. ABC knows what America wants and America wants the marathon in prime time— no matter how it affects the mar-

athoners—and that is how it will be. Ironic. The marathon's own proud history turned out to be its undoing here. (Irony, Part II: The Olympic women's marathon, the first ever, will get an 8 A.M. start.) So the athletes must come prepared. No problem. Alberto Salazar, America's best hope for a gold, says he has figured out how to train for L.A. "I'll start the car in the garage and run in there," he says.

Olympic officials tried to make amends by winding the first 30 kilometers of the course along the blue Pacific, starting at Santa Monica College, then cruising Santa Monica Pier and the fashionable crowd at Marina del Rey. "If they pray hard, they may get a cool breeze there," Henderson says. But even a cool breeze is of little help, since it will most likely be blowing at the runners' backs and won't cool them down appreciably. Then the runners turn inland toward Culver City and what awaits them there is the beginning of the final 10 kilometers, the tough part, and almost all of it through the decaying neighborhoods of West-Central L.A., leading to the Coliseum and the finish line.

Records? If it's hot, forget it. Even though ten men broke 2 hours 10 minutes in the first six months of 1983 alone, Waldemar Cierpinski's Olympic record of 2:09:55 (Montreal, 1976) may even be safe. The heat, the smog, the hilly and slow course should protect it. The Olympic marathon is not of records, anyway. It is of winning, pure and elegant. It is the ultimate race among the world's truest distance runners. Or, as Salazar says, "If you run the marathon, this is it." For Salazar, this may, indeed, be it. Though he is young (he will be twenty-six for the Games), he has suffered through a year of discontent. After winning every marathon he had entered (three New York and one Boston), Salazar has done nothing but lose since early 1983. Worse, he is not a good hot-weather runner. In 1978 at the Falmouth Road Race, he collapsed from heat exhaustion with a 107-degree body temperature.

No, the winner figures to be a man who has leathered his lungs in heat. Take, for instance, Australia's Rob de Castella. De Castella trains in Sydney, where the climate is much like L.A.'s.

Smart money might be on the hero still unseen—a man nobody has heard of. It could be an African, perhaps, one who thinks 42 kilometers in 84 August degrees is a jog to the corner store. Running sage Arthur Lydiard says that man could be Tanzania's Juma Ikangaa and Lydiard picks him to win. There's also Joseph Nzau (pronounced N-Zow), who trains in the lunar landscape of

Laramie, Wyoming, but grew up in Kenya. And then there's Simeon Kigen of Kenya, an unknown until the Chicago Marathon, where he finished second in his first try at the distance. But if an African is to win, he will have to quiet his frayed nerves. The Africans tend to run hair-triggered, eager to punish the field from the very gun. In doing so, they often fade at the close. If one can strap himself down for 30 kilometers, he can win.

But do not forget the East German Cierpinski, who could become the first man to win three straight Olympic marathons. He won in Montreal and again in Moscow in 1980, without U.S. competition, but has raced rarely since. He is a mysterious figure who seems to turn up every four years and win the gold. Cierpinski will be thirty-four for the race, but then again, he finished only 34 seconds off a gold in the world championships marathon in August, 1983, at Helsinki.

And then there is the cast of thousands: the great Japanese runner Toshihiko Seko; the longshot Americans (Bill Rodgers, Dick Beardsley and Greg Meyer); the Brit, Hugh Jones; and the New Zealander, Rod Dixon, who won at New York in 1983 in his first marathon. All of them will have to have a sense of marathon history, a bizarre taste for punishment and an innate desire to be first.

Above: *In the Fukuoka International Marathon of 1983, Toshihiko Seko of Japan—who had won the race three times previously—swept the field in 2:08:52, outdistancing countryman Soh, the Tanzanian runner Ikanga as well as Alberto Salazar of the U.S. Seko once took a Boston Marathon from Bill Rodgers in 1981. Photo by Kishimoto Corp.*

Left: *Takeshi Soh (30) leads America's Alberto Salazar in the Fukuoka International Marathon of 1983. Photo by Kishimoto Corp.*

WOMEN'S MARATHON

BY MARLENE CIMONS

The year as 1896. The name she used was Melpomene, the Greek muse of tragedy. On that day, she crashed the Olympic Games to become the first woman ever to run the marathon, then a distance of 24.9 miles. She finished in 4 hours 30 minutes and then disappeared, never to be seen again.

No woman has run an Olympic marathon since.

But on August 5, the 1984 Los Angeles Games will have a women's marathon, the first ever in Olympic history. Women from all over the world will race 26 miles 385 yards, now the standard marathon distance.

It has been nearly a century since Melpomene's feat, a period in which the development of women's marathon running has seen struggle and confrontation, a startling rise in the participation of women in distance events and dramatic improvements in their performances.

"I saw some of the first women run marathons—and now they're on the verge of running in the Olympics," said Joe Henderson, former executive director of the International Runners Committee, a group organized in 1979 to lobby for a full slate of women's running events in the Olympic Games and a group instrumental in getting approval of a marathon for the Los Angeles Games. "I feel like I'm at Kitty Hawk watching the Wrights take off, or watching people walk on the moon. It's the same feeling."

Despite a decade in which the number of women running marathons worldwide grew from about 20 in 1970 to 8,000 by 1979 (and burgeoned to 15,000 in the United States alone in 1982), it took a substantial amount of persuasion, politicking and hard work to convince the International Olympic Committee and the International Amateur Athletic Federation (IAAF)—the global governing body for track and field—that women could run marathons.

Finally, in February, 1981, the IOC announced that a women's marathon had been added to the 1984 Games.

Women came to distance running late, in part because they had never had the same opportunities to compete as men, and in part because they were held back by old notions that they were too frail and delicate, or that their reproductive systems would be irreparably damaged. But they continued to run. And as the sport caught on, the stereotypes began to fall. So did the records, one after another.

Twenty-one years ago, for example, the women's world record marathon time was 3 hours 37 minutes 7 seconds, set by American Mary Lepper in Culver City, California, on May 16, 1963. In those days, 3:37:07 was considered a very good performance for a woman. Very few women were running marathons and most marathons barred them from entering.

Three years later, in 1966, Roberta Gibb, defying the rules, became the first woman known to have run the prestigious Boston Marathon. She traveled from California, where she was living, hid in the bushes near the starting line, and jumped in when the gun went off. She covered the distance in about 3:20.

A year later, Kathrine Switzer—today the director of sports programs for a cosmetics company and a significant voice for women's running—entered the Boston Marathon as "K. V. Switzer," obtained a number, and managed to finish the race despite a well-publicized clash with race officials along the course.

Australian Adrienne Beams became the first woman to break 3 hours with a 2:46:30 in a marathon in Werribee, Australia, in 1971. American Beth Bonner was the first to break 3 hours in the United States, running 2:55:22 in New York City that same year.

In 1972, women marathoners were sanctioned by the Amateur Athletic Union (now The Athletics Congress), the U.S. governing body for track and field. The same year, women were allowed to run at Boston.

In 1975, American Jacqueline Hansen became the first woman to run under 2:40, clocking a 2:38:19. Women's marathon times were plummeting, and at a pace much faster than the men's.

It took a dozen years before Australian Derek Clayton's world record of 2:08:34, set in 1969, was broken by Alberto Salazar with a 2:08:13 in the 1981 New York City Marathon. In the twelve years from 1971 until 1983, women's world record marathon times dropped by nearly 25 minutes.

Norwegian Grete Waitz, long known as a top middle-distance runner, decided to try a marathon in 1978 and ran a 2:32:29 in her first effort. Since then, she has dominated the event, regularly running sub-2:30 races, including her best, a 2:25:29, in April, 1983, in London.

But it was American Joan Benoit, a Maine native and former Boston University women's track coach, who shocked the running world with her performance in the 1983 Boston Marathon. On a cool day with a slight tailwind, near-perfect marathon conditions, she broke the women's world record by nearly three minutes, running a 2:22:43.

Her time would have won the Olympic gold medal in every men's marathon until 1960.

"The record can definitely go lower," she said. "And I think I can go even faster."

At least eleven women, including Benoit and Waitz, have broken the 2:30 barrier and are contenders for Olympic medals. They include the U.S.'s Julie Brown, who ran a 2:26:26 in June, 1983, in Los Angeles along the Olympic marathon course; New Zealand's Allison Roe, who held the world record of 2:25:29, set in the 1981 New York City Marathon, until Waitz equaled it in London and Benoit broke it at Boston; the U.S.'s Patti Lyons Catalano, former American record-holder who has been battling injuries for the last several years, but hopes to make a comeback; New Zealand's Lorraine Moller and Mary O'Connor; West Germany's Charlotte Teske; Ireland's Carey May; England's Joyce Smith; and Canada's Jacqueline Gareau.

Melpomene would have been proud.

Allison Roe of New Zealand broke the New York City Marathon record with a time of 2:25:28 in 1981. In 1984 she can run an Olympic marathon for the first time. AP Laserphoto

Above: *Julie Brown, famous for her second-place finishes, gained new respect with a 2:26:24 in this marathon victory on the Olympic course in 1983. Photo by Martha Hartnett/ Los Angeles Times*

Far left: *At UCLA in 1975 Julie Brown was winning two-mile races easily. Nine years later she had lengthened her stride to the marathon. Photo by Rick Meyer/ Los Angeles Times*

Left: *Winner's wreath awaits Grete Waitz of Norway as she crosses the finish line at 2:28:09 in the marathon at the world championships in Helsinki, Finland. Waitz is the woman to beat in the event she has ruled for five years. Photo by Woodfin Camp Assoc.*

DECATHLON

BY MIKE LITTWIN

If there's one event that is quintessentially Olympian, it's the decathlon. Every four years, the best decathletes come together and the winner leaves town with the title of World's Greatest Athlete. You can't beat the title. It's just about as good as the gold medal and certainly worth a lot more in terms of cold, hard cash. But for all the fuss made about it, the decathlon is also among the least-watched Olympic track and field events.

Even Bruce Jenner, once the World's Greatest Athlete himself, concedes that viewing the two-day, ten-event tribute to masochism is not unlike "watching paint dry." Not that Jenner is complaining. He turned his Olympic gold into real gold, millions of dollars' worth. If the World's Greatest Athlete happens also to be an American, as used to be the case more often than not, he has a chance to be the World's Richest Athlete.

If it's fame you're after, you can go all the way back to the original decathlon in 1912, when the legend began. Jim Thorpe was the winner that year in Stockholm and King Gustav wanted to crown him—what else?—the World's Greatest Athlete.

The parade of champions is impressive, from Thorpe to Bob Mathias to Rafer Johnson to Jenner. Most of them would later find their faces on boxes of breakfast cereal. Of the sixteen Olympic decathlons, Americans have won ten, but there is no U.S. contender worth noting in Los Angeles in 1984. In fact, aside from Jenner's gold in 1976, the U.S. hasn't won a medal in the decathlon since 1968.

The decathlon's ten events include 100 meters, long jump, shot put, high jump, 400 meters, 110-meter hurdles, discus, pole vault, javelin and 1,500 meters.

The scoring is done according to a complicated table in which times and distances are rewarded with a set number of points. For example, a 10.5 in the 100 meters is worth 932 points, while an 11.1 is worth 780. After two grueling days, it can come down to a real test of fortitude in the final event, the 1,500 meters, in which every second is worth about 10 points.

This year, there may be another great story in the making. Defending Olympic champion Daley Thompson of Great Britain will take on world record-holder Jurgen Hingsen of West Germany. They've been swapping the record for a few years now, but in head-to-head competition it has been all Thompson.

In five meetings, Thompson has won them all, including last year's world championships in Helsinki, Finland. "I've always said that winning is more important than records," Thompson said afterward. Thompson's best mark is 8,734 points; Hingsen's record is 8,777. They're the two best of all time, and just to add a little spice to the confrontation, they don't much like each other, either.

"It's very important for me to beat Daley," Hingsen said after losing in Helsinki. "Everyone says he's unbeatable, that he's untouchable. Nobody is untouchable, especially in the decathlon." Thompson hasn't lost since 1978. Ask him if he's a bad loser, he says, smiling, "I can't remember."

Thompson is an engaging athlete with a ready smile, a ready joke and a thick Cockney accent. He laughs his way through the controversies that always seem to be raging about him. By his own admission, he enjoys a little controversy almost as much as he enjoys competing. And the British tabloids have made him one of their favorites.

Hingsen recently married a California woman from Santa Barbara—putting to rest his playboy image—and they're now celebrities in West Germany. Hingsen is 6-foot-7, blue-eyed, muscular, agile and bright. They also call him the German Hercules. And Hingsen, who speaks very good English, has professed an interest in acting. Call him Hollywood Hingsen.

But the personalities will be secondary to performance on the Coliseum floor, although Thompson loves to joke around while he's performing and maybe psych out his opponent along the way. Said Hingsen: "I don't pay any attention to him."

You can't do too much fooling around and be a decathlete. It requires six hours of training, six days a week. A decathlon is so taxing that it is virtually impossible to compete for six weeks after completing one. Says Thompson: "I enjoy the training. It beats having to go to work."

It's hard to tell upon which event the matchup will turn. In Helsinki, Hingsen lost to Thompson on the first day when he developed leg cramps during the high jump. Hingsen, who usually does around 7 feet, jumped only 6-6. Look for Thompson to win the sprints (he runs a legitimate 9.5 in the 100) and for Hingsen to win the strength events. Hingsen has a real edge in a few events, especially the javelin. Thompson, though, is a far better pole vaulter, and that could make the difference. Hingsen has a simple game plan: "I try to beat Daley in every event."

Normally, the decathlon is a race with the clock or the tape measure. But, this time, it's Thompson vs. Hingsen, and it should be fun. You may not watch much of it, but you'll probably care who wins. As Jenner says, "They only have one good meet every four years, but that's a real good one."

In the women's version, the seven-event heptathlon, the East Germans are favored. They took the top three spots in Helsinki, with Ramona Neubert the winner. That's not exactly a surprise. Neubert came into the 1984 season as the world record-holder who has never been beaten. American Jane Frederick has an outside shot at a medal.

Daley Thompson, here throwing the discus, is attempting to become the second man to win the Olympic decathlon twice. The other: Bob Mathias of the U.S. Photo by Woodfin Camp Assoc.

Decathlon gold medalist Daley Thompson of Great Britain clocks 10.62 seconds in winning the 100-meter dash at Moscow in 1980. Georg Werthner of Austria, on the right, finished fourth overall. AP Wirephoto

FIELD EVENTS

BY ALAN GREENBERG

For many years, the United States dominated track and field in the world. In Olympic competition, it wasn't at all unusual to see U.S. athletes sweeping the gold, silver and bronze medals at a single event. Those days are gone.

Since the emergence of the Eastern European countries in post–World War II competition and the entry of the Soviet Union at the 1952 Helsinki Olympics, the U.S. standing in the field events has eroded faster than any beachfront, swept away by a tide of foreign athletes with long surnames and even longer throws and jumps. Indeed, the U.S. has reached such a low ebb in the field events that it is favored to win a gold medal in only one. In fact, there are only a few events in which U.S. competitors may win even one medal, any medal. As the 1983 world championships at Helsinki showed, the top prospects for Olympic medals in the field events are a blend of proven foreign veterans and newcomers, some unknown just one year earlier.

Men's High Jump—The event is in a state of flux. At Helsinki, six men cleared 7 feet 6 inches, but it was the relatively unknown Gennady Avdeyenko of the Soviet Union who won the gold with a personal best of 7-7¼. Tyke Peacock of the U.S. was second, also at 7-7¼, equaling the U.S. record. He upped it to 7-7¾ a week later in West Berlin. World record-holder Zhu Jianhua of China, who held the world record at 7-9¼ prior to Helsinki, was third at 7-6. He broke his own record a month later, jumping 7-9¾. Zhu, however, has very limited international experience. At least five other jumpers could win a medal, including European champion Dietmar Mogenburg (7-8½) and Carlo Thranhardt (7-8), both of West Germany; Valery Serada (7-8½) and Igor Paklin (7-7¾), both of the USSR, and Milt Ottey of Canada (7-7¼), who broke his ankle at the start of the 1983 indoor season after winning the 1982 NCAA title. Dwight Stones, a tough competitor, is the second best U.S. jumper, but his 7-7¼ best leaves him a notch below the world elite.

Men's Pole Vault—Despite the fanfare about the U.S.'s Billy Olson and his world indoor record of 19-0¼ and the world record performances by flying Frenchmen Thierry Vigneron (19-1½) and Pierre Quinon (19-1), it's the Soviets who are the most consistent in the big meets. At Helsinki, little-known Sergei Bubka vaulted a personal best of 18-8½, upsetting Konstantin Volkov, the sil-

ver medalist at the Moscow Olympics. Volkov was second at 18-4¼. Despite finishing tenth at Helsinki, the USSR's Vladimir Polyakov, who was the world record-holder at 19-0¾, is still a threat. Other medal possibilities are Atanas Tarev of Bulgaria (18-6½); the Polish duo of 1976 Olympic gold medalist Tadeusz Slusarski (18-8½) and Wladimir Kozakiewicz, the gold medalist four years later with a then-world record 18-11; and Patrick Bhoni of Switzerland and San Jose State (18-8¼).

Men's Long Jump—When you say Carl Lewis, you've said it all. He represents the U.S.'s best chance for a gold medal in an individual field event. He has the world's best mark at sea level—28-10¼, just over four inches less than Bob Beamon's 29-2½ in 1968 at Mexico City. Lewis last lost at the 1980 U.S. Olympic trials. The U.S. swept this event at Helsinki and could do it again at Los Angeles, but it won't be easy. Larry Myricks (28-1), Jason Grimes (27-6½) and Mike Conley (27-2) will fight for the two remaining spots on the U.S. team. Olympic champion Lutz Dombrowski of East Germany (28-0½), who missed the 1983 season with a broken leg, is a real medal threat. Others are Laszlo Szalma of Hungary (26-11), Nenad Stekic of Yugoslavia (27-8¾ in 1975) and Sergei Rodin of the USSR (27-4).

Men's Triple Jump—Wide open. Zdzislaw Hoffman of Poland came out of nowhere to win the world championships with a personal best of 57-2. Britain's Keith Connor was the best jumper in 1982, winning the NCAA, European and Commonwealth titles, but was slightly injured in 1983. The U.S.'s Willie

Banks (57-7½) was the best jumper in 1981. Gennady Valukevich (57-2) and Alexander Beskrovny (57-6½) are the Soviets' best, but both performed badly at Helsinki. Additional medal threats are Ken Lorraway of Australia (57-3½), Ajayi Agbebaku of Nigeria (56-7½), third at Helsinki, and Conley (56-6½), fourth at Helsinki.

Men's Shot Put—Udo Beyer of East Germany is the world's best, but he finished only third at the Moscow Olympics and fifth at Helsinki, where he was slightly injured. He's still the favorite, with a world record 72-10¾ at the U.S.-East Germany meet in Los Angeles in 1983. The U.S.'s Dave Laut, fourth at Helsinki, is a definite medal threat. Edward Sarul won with 70-2¼ at Helsinki, one of the all-time best throws at a meet where there was dope-testing. His personal record is 71-1½. Youngsters Ulf Timmerman of East Germany (70-1) and Remigius Machura of Czechoslovakia were second and third, respectively, at Helsinki and threw close to their bests. Janis Bojars (69-11) is the best of the Soviets.

Men's Discus—Imrich Bugar of Czechoslovakia and Luis Delis of Cuba, the No. 1 and 2 finishers at Helsinki, tend to perform well in meets where dope-testing is done and conditions aren't always favorable. Bugar, 1980 Moscow silver medalist and 1982 European champion, has a best of 232-0. Delis, the 1980 bronze medalist, has thrown 233-2. The U.S. has long throwers who have not performed well in big meets. Former Olympic champion Mac Wilkins and John Powell, both former world record-holders, didn't finish

in the top eight at Helsinki, despite having 1983 bests of 230-10 and 224-1, respectively. Ben Plucknett had a 237-4 in 1981 that was never ratified as a world record because he was found to have taken an illegal substance. Art Burns's top throw is 233-6, but he finished eighth at Helsinki with 207-5. The USSR's Yuri Dumchev is the current world record-holder, but he's been even less successful than the U.S. throwers in top competition.

Men's Hammer—The Soviets swept the field in Moscow and could do so again in Los Angeles. Yuri Syedikh (268-4) has won virtually every European and Olympic title since 1976. Teammate and current world record-holder Sergei Litvinov (276-0) upset him at Helsinki. Igor Nikulin, with a best of 274-1, was fourth for the USSR at Helsinki, with Poland's Zdzislaw Kwasny slipping in to take third. West and East Germany each have outside medal threats. Dave McKenzie (244-5) and Ed Burke (243-1) are the best U.S. throwers.

Men's Javelin—The U.S.'s Tom Petranoff, who set a world record 327-2 in 1983, is a real gold medal threat. Detlef Michel of East Germany, who beat Petranoff for first at Helsinki, is a consistent thrower with a 317-4 best. The Soviets are strong with Dainis Kula (302-0) and Heino Puuste (309-1). Finland has two threats in Pentti Sinersarri (307-5) and Arto Harkonen (298-8). The U.S.'s Bob Roggy (314-4) was best in the world in 1982, but he was bothered by minor injuries in 1983.

Women's High Jump—The USSR's Tamara Bykova is favored. Her 6-7 won

at Helsinki. A few weeks later, she set a 6-8¼ world record. West Germany's Ulrike Meyfarth (6-8) and the U.S.'s Louise Ritter, who set a U.S. record of 6-7 and finished third in Helsinki, are a cut above the rest. Colleen Sommer (6-6¾ indoors) and Pam Spencer (6-5½) make this U.S. women's best field event. Other threats are Cuba's Silvia Costa and Soviet Larisa Kositsyna Poluiko, both with 6-6 bests. Don't count out Italy's Sara Simeoni (6-7¼), the 1980 Olympic gold medalist injured during Helsinki qualifying.

Women's Long Jump—East Germany's Heike Daute (23-5¼) and Romania's Anisorara Cusmir (24-4¼) are the best. Daute, only eighteen, won at Helsinki. Cusmir is the world record-holder. Carol Lewis (22-10½), younger sister of Carl, beat the East Germans in East Germany in 1982 and was third at Helsinki. The Soviets have three 23-foot jumpers and Britain's Beverly Kinch (22-7¾) could also be a factor. U.S. record-holder Jodi Anderson (22-11¾) may be in the picture.

Women's Shot Put—East Germany's Ilona Slupianek (73-6) is the world record-holder and Moscow gold medalist, who didn't win at Helsinki probably because of a slight injury. Helen Fibingerova of Czechoslovakia won the 1983 world title at the age of thirty-four and holds the indoor record (73-9¾). As for the Americans, forget it.

Women's Discus—Eastern Europeans dominate. Gisela Beyer (232-10) and Martina Opitz (230-6), the Helsinki winner, lead the East Germans. Both will be at Los Angeles. Irina Meszynski is also a threat with a 1982 throw of 234-3.

Bulgaria's Maria (235-7) and Tsvetana Christova (231-9) were third and fourth, respectively, at Helsinki. The USSR's Galina Murashova (225-11) was second at Helsinki, upstaging teammate Galina Savinkova, the world record-holder at 240-4. Leslie Deniz is the U.S. record-holder at 213-1.

Women's Javelin—Performances in this event have improved dramatically since the U.S.'s Kate Schmidt set a world record of 227-5 in 1977. Finland's Tiina Lillak won at Helsinki and has upped the record to 245-3. Greece's Sofia Sakorafa (243-5) set a world record in 1982 but wasn't at Helsinki. Reportedly, she was injured then but threw well after the championships. East Germans Antje Kempe (232-11) and Petra Felke (226-5) are definite medal threats, as are Britain's Fatima Whitbread (228-2) and Tessa Sanderson (241-5), second and fourth, respectively, at Helsinki. Anna Veroli of Italy (232-7) won the 1982 European championships and was third at Helsinki. Fausta Quintavalla of Italy (220-8) is an outside threat, as is Antoaneta Todorova of Bulgaria, who set a world record of 235-10 in 1981 while still a teen-ager. The U.S.'s best appear to be Karin Smith (212-6) and Schmidt, who is expected to compete again.

Opposite: *Finnish javelin thrower Tiina Lillak was undefeated in 1983 and won a gold medal in the world championships at Helsinki, FInland. She holds the pending world record at 245 feet 3 inches — amazingly, just over 100 feet longer than Babe Didrickson's winning throw in the 1932 games. Photo by Woodfin Camp Assoc.*

Far left: *Tom Petranoff, preparing to unloose a throw, added nearly 10 feet to the world javelin record with a toss of 327 feet 2 inches. In the background is another top U.S. javelin prospect, Bob Roggy. Photo by Jose Galvez/Los Angeles Times*

Left: *American Rod Ewaliko won the javelin at the U.S.A./Mobil Outdoors in 1983 but was over 40 feet short of Petranoff's world record. Photo by Patrick Downs/Los Angeles Times*

Above left: *Polish triple jumper Zdzislaw Hoffman leaped from 75th place on the world list in 1982 to a world championship in 1983. He saved his best for the biggest meet: 57 feet 2 inches. Photo by Woodfin Camp Assoc.*

Above right: *Willie Banks is the best triple jumper in the U.S. and second in the world to the current world champion— Hoffman. Banks, however, jumped farther than Hoffman's Helsinki best in the U.S.A./ Mobil outdoor games in 1983. Photo by Jayne Kamin/Los Angeles Times*

Left: *Officials do what officials do at track and field meets. They study the ground a lot—and then they measure the throw, or rule on a foul jump. Photo by Joe Kennedy/Los Angeles Times*

Opposite: *Carl Lewis soars past 28 feet, a distance that has become routine for the world long jump champion even though it has been achieved by few others in track history. Photo by Jose Galvez/ Los Angeles Times*

Ilona Slupianek, the East German
powerhouse, muscles the shot beyond 71
feet in a dual meet with U.S. Slupianek set
a world record of 73-8 in 1980. Photo by
Joe Kennedy/Los Angeles Times

American women simply do not measure
up to the East Europeans in the shot put,
but Denise Wood (269) is among the
U.S.'s best. Photo by Joe Kennedy/
Los Angeles Times

Looking quite boyish, a 20-year-old Al Oerter (right) turned up at the 1956 Melbourne Games and won the gold. In three more Olympics Oerter came in first, extending his distance 27 feet by 1968. Passing up the Games in 1972 and 1976, Oerter came in fourth at the trials for 1980 but, of course, no American competed. However, at age 47, in 1983 (above), he was back on form at a U.S.-East German meet in Los Angeles. Photo by Patrick Downs/Los Angeles Times

Despite her anguish here, Louise Ritter has a 6-5 jump in 1983, 3¹/₄ inches short of the world record but closing. Photo by Patrick Downs/Los Angeles Times

Early in 1984, America's Billy Olson vaulted over 19 feet indoors. So did the Soviet's Sergei Bubka. The Olympic jump-off should be a thriller. Photo by Patrick Downs/Los Angeles Times

Among the world's top field hockey teams: India vs. Pakistan at the All-Asia Final in 1983. Photo by Kishimoto Corp.

Soccer at the National Sports Festival at Indianapolis in 1983 offered American collegians a chance to perform for Olympic coaches. Photo by David Madison/Focus on Sports

Cuba played the U.S. at the Pan Am Games in 1983, a match-up that will likely repeat in the Olympics. Photo by Focus on Sports

Team handball, unfamiliar to most Americans, resembles indoor soccer but the ball is thrown, not kicked. Photo by Kishimoto Corp.

Pre-Olympic volleyball matches at Long Beach in 1983 pitted Japan against China *(top)* and the U.S. *(above)*. Photo by Kishimoto Corp.

Michael Jordan (5) and other U.S. collegians ganged up against Brazil in the 1983 Pan Am Games. Photo by Focus on Sports

MEN'S BASKETBALL

BY MARK HEISLER

Rome fell, Britannia no longer rules the waves nor the Democrats the South. Nothing is forever, not even the United States's domination of Olympic basketball, which is now threatened by men from playgrounds in Moscow, Belgrade and Milan.

The U.S. has already lost one Olympic basketball game and the 1972 gold medal that went with it. The Soviet Union is now being afforded a chance for an encore in Los Angeles, but this time on merit, without benefit of extra chances afforded them by questionable officiating decisions.

A young Soviet team, with only about half of the national roster, played impressively on a tour of U.S. campuses in the fall of 1982, losing only to national powers Kentucky and Virginia. Virginia won only after a referee's call put Ralph Sampson at the free-throw line in the closing seconds with a chance to tie the game and send it into overtime. Bill Wall, the American offical who put the tour together, later remarked that the call had been horrible. "And I hired the referee," he said. Despite hometown calls, a hectic schedule and everything else that went with playing on the road, the Soviets went 6-2.

There is even some question that the USSR will be the toughest challenger. The Soviets finished third to Yugoslavia and Italy in their own Olympics in 1980. Shortly after their 1982 tour of the U.S., they finished third in Europe behind the Italians and the Spaniards. Bob Knight, who'll coach the U.S. team, says that he would love to take the Italian team into the NCAA tournament.

The Soviet tour stunned U.S. coaches. If no Tartar version of Julius Erving has yet been unveiled, it showed that there are now foreign guards who can handle the toughest full-court pressure applied by their quickest American counterparts. CBS commentator Billy Packer says Soviet point guard Valdis Valters would be an All-American, if only he were an American.

The foreign big men, who used to lurch around much to the amusement of their American counterparts, have been replaced by the likes of Soviet 7-footer Arvidas Sabonis, who was eighteen on the U.S. tour, when American coaches started calling him the best young big man in the world. Foreign teams have other advantages: They're older and more physically mature than the collegians who make up the U.S. team; they play together all year every year instead of a few months every four years; some of their best players may make from fifty to one hundred thousand dollars playing ball in Europe, but they're still "amateurs"; the best Americans play in the NBA, which makes them "professionals" and thus ineligible.

Nevertheless, it's a little early to relegate the U.S. to longshot status. There isn't a basketball coach in the world, including the Soviet Union's Alexander Gomelski, who makes anyone but the U.S. the favorite, especially in front of a home crowd in the Los Angeles Forum. But it isn't the way it was.

Basketball first appeared in an Olympics in 1904, in St. Louis, only thirteen years after Dr. James Naismith invented the game. It was a "demonstration sport," as much to the Americans as the rest of the world. In St. Louis, the first Olympic court was laid out on the infield of a baseball diamond.

That did it until 1936, the Berlin Olympics, better remembered for Jesse Owens and Adolf Hitler, when basketball returned to stay, but still on an outdoor clay court—almost as if it were tennis. The Germans had gone big for these Games, building lavish bungalows to house the athletes. They even reconstructed one of the humbler bungalows used by athletes at the Los Angeles Games in 1932 to point up the contrast. They ringed the main basketball court with low cement walls and built stands behind them. However, a drenching rain fell on the day of the final between the U.S. and Canada. The walls held the water in, turning the court into a mud bath and then a wading pool.

"If you dribbled the ball," says Sam Balter, a member of the U.S. team, now a retired Los Angeles sportscaster, "it splashed and floated away. The press gave it no attention whatsoever. I got home and read the clippings and there was nothing about it. Didn't anybody think it was funny, a 19-8 game between the best players in the world? Dr. Naismith was there. After the game, he made a little speech and gave us laurel wreaths. He said that his dream had come true, that skills were being demonstrated on the highest level, and we just looked at each other. That was probably the worst exhibition we'd ever seen anywhere. We really had no competition. One of our good high school teams could have won. Mexico and Canada had pretty good teams. Maybe they were as good as a fair college team. We scrimmaged the Germans. No one kept score, but if they had, I think it would have been about 90-0."

For the record, the first U.S. victory came over Spain—by a score of 2-0. The Spanish Civil War had just broken out and the Spaniards forfeited.

After that, things rolled along nicely for the U.S. In every Olympics, they'd win eight games, pick up their gold medals and go home. If they played well, it was no contest. In 1948 in London, for example, they beat France, 65-21, in the final. If they went to sleep, they'd win narrowly. In the same year, they beat Argentina, 59-57.

The Soviets are nothing if not fast learners, and in 1952, in Helsinki, they made the finals for the first time. This is the report of Howard Hobson, the U.S. basketball chairman:

"The drawing saw our team matched with Russia in the very first game of the second round. The word traveled fast. The game was moved to Messenhalli II, a hall where a larger crowd could be accommodated. More than four thousand spectators jammed the pavilion. Several times as many spectators would have been glad to pay the top price of five dollars to see this game. Both teams were undefeated. Russia was favored by most of the Iron Curtain countries. They were supposed to be undefeated in more than nine hundred games and confidently expected to win.

"Our boys were really keyed for this one. The pre-game spectacle was dramatic and thrilling. . . . The Russian captain stepped forward and presented our captain, Dan Pippin, with a beautiful Russian banner. Our players rushed over and shook hands with the Russians. Our players lost little time in demonstrating our superiority to the big Red team of Russia. Almost immediately, we went out to a 10-point lead. The game was only ten minutes old when the Russians' star center, Otar Korkiaa, 6-5, came out second best in a collision with Clyde Lovellette and was carried from the floor. . . . Fine sportsmanship prevailed and the teams had their pictures taken together following the game. Our final score was 86-58."

By 1956 in Melbourne, the Soviets had a big man of their own, 7-foot-3 Jan Kruminish, a woodcutter from the Ukraine. Grace was not Kruminish's forte. Terry Dischinger, an American who'd played against him, said Kruminish stepped on a Brazilian player's foot and broke it. Crowds used to jeer him, but Kruminish always displayed the same big, toothy smile. "I do not mind the people," he said. "If I play good, they like me. If I play bad, they don't."

He was matched in 1956 against the first big Olympic star, Bill Russell, just out of the University of San Francisco, NCAA two-time champion. Russell was beyond anything the Soviets had ever seen. He led the U.S. to the traditional 8-0, joined the Boston Celtics and led them to eleven titles in his thirteen seasons. After that, the Olympics became a springboard to NBA stardom. "Bill had the Russians so psyched that I'd almost swear they were trying to foul out," said Olympic teammate Birdie Haldorson. "Then they'd go to the sidelines, get their cameras and take pictures of Bill."

Four years later, in Rome, the U.S. unveiled the so-called "greatest team ever assembled," with Jerry Lucas, Oscar Robertson and Jerry West. John Havlicek and Satch Sanders didn't even make the cut. The "greatest team" compliment was probably excessive. An NBA team might have trashed the Americans, but nobody in the Olympics was going to. The U.S. averaged 102 points a game and held opponents to 60. They held Kruminish scoreless. In the final, they took leads of 16-2 and 41-14 against Brazil and won, 90-63. Robertson, Lucas, Walt Bellamy and Dischinger would all be NBA rookies of the year. West and Robertson would make the Hall of Fame. Lucas was a many-time NBA all-star, as was Bellamy. Bob Boozer and Darrall Imhoff had long NBA careers.

"Back then," says Pete Newell, the coach, "the favorite sons of the Olympic team were the track people. We had a train ride from Milan to Rome. The track guys got to ride first-class and they put us back in steerage. Here I am, with Oscar and Jerry, the two greatest players of them all, and we're riding with the goats, pigs and chickens."

In Tokyo in 1964, Gomelski, the Soviet coach, declared: "There will be a surprise for everyone. We are fed up with second." Then his team lost, 73-59, in the final to a U.S. team led by Luke Jackson and Bill Bradley. In 1968 in Mexico City, the U.S. was without Kareem Abdul-Jabbar (then Lew Alcindor), who stayed home to honor the black protest of the games. An unknown nineteen-year-old named Spencer Haywood, the youngest player ever to make the U.S. team, became the star in his stead. The U.S. sailed on, dropping Yugoslavia and Kresimir Cosic, who'd played college ball at Brigham Young, 65-50, in the final.

In 1972 in Munich, the U.S. won its first seven games, running its Olympic record to 63-0. Then it met the Soviets in the final—and lost, 51-50, although the U.S. Olympic committee has never conceded that. The U.S. had taken a 50-49 lead on Doug Collins's two free throws

with :03 left. The Soviets were then allowed three chances to put the ball in play, after protests that the clock had been improperly set. On the third attempt, guard Ivan Edeshenko threw a length-of-the-court pass to the Soviet star, 6-foot-7 Alexander Belov, once drafted by the New Orleans Jazz. Belov stepped between (charged into, claimed the U.S.) Jim Forbes and Kevin Joyce and dunked. There went the neighborhood. Many protests followed, but they were disallowed. The U.S. team didn't show up to claim its silver medals.

Four years later in Montreal, a team led by Adrian Dantley, Phil Ford and Scott May went 8-0, but the old awe was gone. The U.S. played Yugoslavia twice, beating it by 19 points, then by 21 in the final, after which Yugoslav forward Vinko Jelovac said: "Russia was the best team in this tournament. We knew we could beat Russia, but beating Russia and the U.S.A. in two straight nights is not possible."

Four years later, the U.S. boycotted the Moscow Games. Four years after that, the amateur basketball world has drawn closer.

In 1981, Stuart Gray (left) *and Pat Ewing* (opposite) *were both considered stars of the future in basketball and likely leaders of the U.S. team in 1984. Today, only Ewing is considered a heavyweight. Photos by Bob Chamberlin/Los Angeles Times*

Greg Dreiling of Wichita State,
Kansas, goes for a shot. Photo by Bob
Chamberlin/Los Angeles Times

WOMEN'S BASKETBALL

BY CHRIS COBBS

Women have been playing basketball for nearly one hundred years, and now the skilled and exciting Cheryl Miller, USC's effervescent 6-foot-2 forward, is quietly telling people she expects to be the first woman to dunk a shot in a game. In the Olympics, no less! Talk about coming a long way, baby.

But the promise of a spectacular individual feat is secondary to another piece of history that could unfold in Los Angeles. The Soviet Union, which has dominated women's basketball on an international level for decades, might just get stuffed by the United States.

Women's basketball in America has made great strides since it was added to the Olympics in 1976, and the U.S. team is poised to make a run at the gold medal.

The sheer athletic talent of Miller and her American teammates pitted against the mechanical excellence of the Soviets, makes the 1984 Olympic women's basketball tournament tremendously interesting. The contrasting styles also illustrate how much the sport has evolved in the last fifteen years. As a result of changes in the rules, the American game has become faster paced, attracting a greater number of skilled athletes, who have in turn transformed the U.S. into a budding world power.

America did not become that kind of power overnight. Billie Moore, now the coach at UCLA, recalled that in her first experience with coaching an American team in international play the U.S. women lost to the Soviets by 55 points in the 1973 World University Games. A player on that team, Pat Head Summitt, will coach the U.S. team in 1984. Thinking back a decade, she said it was pretty much a question then of how badly the Soviets wanted to beat the Americans. In 1976, just three years after that humiliating defeat, Summitt was joined on the U.S. Olympic team by players such as Ann Meyers and Nancy Lieberman, and the result was a silver medal at Montreal. The Americans were coming closer—within 20 points of the Soviets—but they still needed more international experience to be truly competitive.

The U.S. boycott of the 1980 Olympics at Moscow made it impossible to gauge how much improvement had been made since Montreal. But since 1980, American teams have defeated the Soviets twice in exhibitions and narrowly lost last summer in the world championships in Brazil. With a base of thirty to forty experienced and talented players, the U.S. will have its best talent pool ever for 1984 and is expected to be at the forefront of a group of nations challenging the Soviet Union. Other challengers likely will include China, Korea, Cuba and Canada.

The Soviet Union still has the tallest and most potent force in women's basketball in 7-foot-1 center Uliana Semanova. Her presence, plus a rigorous year-round training program, has given the Soviets an aura of invincibility. Their roster also includes half a dozen or more players in the range of 6-4 to 6-8. Moreover, the Soviets have veteran coach Ligya Alekszejeva, who has a systematic approach to rebounding and transition basketball that few teams can disrupt. Alekszejeva has also developed a unique reliance on specialists and role players.

Basketball, a native American sport, is now played in a wide diversity of styles. But until the late 1960s, the U.S. women's version was poky and old-fashioned. In fact, it was hard to distinguish from the very first game held at Smith College on March 22, 1893. Bicycling, badminton and tennis were the main sports in which women participated before James Naismith nailed up his peach basket in Springfield, Massachusetts, in 1891. Some eighteen months later, the women at Smith, having witnessed a game played by men, took to the court in bloomers and long-sleeved blouses. A team of sophomores defeated the freshmen, 5-4. The audience was exclusively female, in deference to the delicate moral code of the day.

Women's basketball in the U.S. didn't enter its modern phase until about the time Miller and her peers were born, in the mid-to-late 1960s. By then, the sport was well established on the international level, and the Soviet Union was already developing taller, stronger women. The game was eventually updated with new rules that made it more attractive to more American women. The new rules allowed deflecting the ball, unlimited dribbling and player movement all over the court. Once these rules were in place, the game became more compelling for spectator and player alike. With the growing popularity of the feminist movement, and with the formation of the Association of Intercollegiate Athletics for Women (AIAW) in 1969, women's basketball in the U.S. took another step forward. The first women's national collegiate championship was held that same year.

Whether the U.S. has come far enough now to challenge the Soviet Union remains to be seen. If there is a U.S. advantage, it would be its feel for the nuances of the game, along with the dazzle and creativity of players such as Miller, Cindy Noble and Lynette Woodard, each expected to play a prominent role on the Olympic team. There is no guarantee that the U.S. will displace the Soviet Union as long as Semanova is active, but the sport of women's basketball should benefit from the interest created by the challenge to Soviet supremacy in 1984.

Soviet giant Uliana Semanova towers over Hungarian players at the 1980 Moscow Olympics in a game her team won 120-62. AP Wirephoto

Opposite: *Twins Paula (11) and Pam McGee (30) helped turn USC into a powerhouse in women's college basketball. Their goal is to do the same for the U.S. in the Olympics. Photo by Bob Chamberlin/Los Angeles Times*

Above right: *Paula McGee—of the twin McGees from USC—shoots a jumper over a defender. The McGees and Cheryl Miller make up USC's Murderess Row, the most formidable front line in women's college basketball. Photo by Bob Chamberlin/Los Angeles Times*

Below right: *Opponents here but probable teammates on the U.S. women's basketball team, Anne Donovan (left) and Cheryl Miller may have to stand on one another's shoulders to stop the 7-foot-2 Soviet Semanova. Photo by Larry Sharkey/Los Angeles Times*

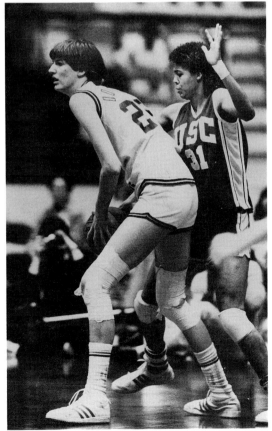

Cheryl Miller, some say, plays her game on a different level. Here she rises above the crowd on a jump shot. She has a chance to be the greatest woman player of them all. Photo by Bob Chamberlin/ Los Angeles Times

VOLLEYBALL

BY JERRY CROWE

Doug Beal and Arie Selinger, respective coaches of the United States men's and women's volleyball teams, expect their teams to win Olympic medals this summer at the Long Beach Arena.

For either team, that would be unprecedented.

In fact, it is noteworthy that the Americans will even be competing, although the U.S. qualified automatically as the host country. It has been sixteen years since the U.S. last participated in Olympic volleyball competition. As Beal said, "We invented the sport, and that's about all we've done."

Yes, volleyball *was* invented in the U.S.—William G. Morgan is credited with introducing the game in 1895 at Springfield College in Massachusetts, the same school where James Naismith invented basketball four years earlier—but you couldn't tell that by the Americans' record in international competition. The game has been refined and nurtured in other parts of the world, most notably the Soviet Union and Japan.

Now, through separate year-round training programs for the men and women in Southern California, the U.S. is trying to catch up. The U.S. Volleyball Association believes a strong showing by U.S. teams this summer will provide a tremendous boost to the sport's popularity in this country. "We're looking at it like the success of the team [at the Olympics] is important to the future of the sport," Beal said.

The timing may be right for the U.S. The U.S. women's team, which includes seven players who were on the team that qualified for the Moscow Games four years ago but was denied a chance to compete because of the boycott, is considered one of the world's strongest. In the spring of last year, Selinger all but guaranteed a gold medal for his team, saying the U.S. had a "95 percent chance" of winning in Los Angeles. Later, he hedged a bit, but he still believes the U.S. has a good chance to unseat the Soviet Union as the Olympic champion. He considers his team one of the gold medal favorites, along with Japan and China.

The core of Selinger's team—Flo Hyman, Rita Crockett, Debbie Green, Laurie Flachmeier, Sue Woodstra, Julie Vollersten and Carolyn Becker—have been training together for five years. Crockett, one of six players named to the all-world team in 1982, and Hyman, at 6-foot-5 one of the world's tallest players, are ranked among the best hitters

in the world. And Green, a 5-foot-4 setter, has been playing volleyball on the international level for ten years. Selinger has been their coach for nine years.

The team reached a high-water mark at the 1982 world championships, a quadrennial event, when it finished third after losing a controversial match to the host country, Peru, in the semifinals. In a preliminary round, the U.S. beat the world champion Chinese, 15-6, 15-9, 15-11, and in the match for third place came back from the loss to Peru to beat Japan. Japan had not placed lower than second in any tournament in twenty years.

The U.S. men's team has not been nearly as successful. But its supporters are quick to point out that it has had a higher mountain to climb. Men's volleyball is not a popular sport in the United States—it has been an NCAA sport only since 1970, and fewer than thirty Division I schools sponsor varsity programs—so Beal is working with a thinner talent pool than Selinger. "I think the people who compare [the two programs] don't have an understanding of the two sports in our society," Beal said. "It's like comparing our men's basketball team with our men's field hockey team. The two sports aren't equal in stature. Volleyball is one of our most popular women's sports. Men's volleyball is struggling for survival."

Despite the handicaps, Beal has put together a team that has beaten all of the top teams in the world except the

Soviet Union, which rarely loses. Of his players, Beal said that Karch Kiraly, a four-time All-American from UCLA, and 6-foot-8 Craig Buck from Pepperdine have developed into two of the best players in the world. But the defending world and Olympic champion Soviets have not lost a major competition since they were upset by Poland in the 1976 Olympic final at Montreal.

Volleyball has come a long way since its inception. The game Morgan designed was primarily for middle-aged men who considered basketball too strenuous. Today, volleyball at the international level is fast-moving and requires tremendous physical ability and endurance.

Bob Beeten, the U.S. Olympic Committee's head trainer, worked with the U.S. women's team when it trained in Colorado Springs for two years. In 1979, he told *Sports Illustrated* that "in terms of overall strength, they are probably the best or among the best" women athletes he had ever tested, "fitter even than the track and field women, with the exception of distance runners."

Volleyball was introduced as an Olympic sport at Tokyo in 1964 and has been dominated ever since by the Soviets and Japanese. Between them, they have won seventeen Olympic medals. The Soviets, whose men's and women's teams have each won three gold medals, have finished lower than second only once. The Japanese women, who won gold medals in 1964 and 1976

Karch Kiraly (31), leader of the U.S. men's volleyball team, is a four-time All-American. He led UCLA to three NCAA championships. Photo by Lou Mack/Los Angeles Times

at Montreal, have never finished lower than second. When Japan boycotted the 1980 Games, the Soviets won both the men's and women's titles.

The rules are basically the same for men and women, although the height of the net for men (7 feet, 11⅝ inches) is 7½ inches higher than for women. The object of the game, quite simply, is to hit the ball over the net into the opponents' side of the court so that they can't return it. Points can be scored only by the serving team. The court itself is 18 meters long (approximately 59 feet) and 9 meters wide (approximately 30 feet). The captain is the only person who can talk to officials during a match. Coaching from the bench is not allowed.

The Olympic men's tournament involves ten teams: host country, world champion, Olympic champion, World Cup champion, zone champions from North and South America, Europe, Asia and Africa, plus a qualifier from an at-large tournament. The eight-team women's tournament involves qualifiers from the same competitions, minus the World Cup and at-large champions.

Below left: *Rita Crockett, who is said to have a vertical leap of 39 inches, goes high for a spike. She's been a mainstay of the U.S. women's volleyball team since 1978 and is All-World.*

Below right: *Julie Vollertsen* (left) *and Jeannie Beauprey (15) follow the bouncing ball in a U.S.-South Korea women's volleyball match.*

Opposite: *Flo Hyman* (left) *and Jeannie Beauprey fail to block Korean striker Kyooko Ishida's spike at a 1983 game. Photos by Leo Jarzomb/Los Angeles Times*

TENNIS

BY MIKE PENNER

New ground was broken, in more ways than one, when the International Olympic Committee voted to include tennis as a demonstration sport in the 1984 Summer Games.

It was broken literally when UCLA began construction on its new Tennis Center, an 8,500-seat facility that will serve as the site of the men's and women's Olympic competitions. And it was broken figuratively when the IOC announced that the tennis exhibition would be open to *all* players twenty years and under—the first time declared professionals have been permitted to participate in any Olympic event.

With tennis scheduled to become a full-fledged sport in the 1988 Summer Games in Seoul, South Korea, some officials see the 1984 tennis demonstration as a possible first step toward the elimination—or at least the softening—of the Olympics' "amateur-only" policy.

"The twenty-and-under open policy represents a middle ground between two schools of thought," said William Burke, commissioner of tennis for the Los Angeles Olympic Organizing Committee. "On one hand, opening the tennis to some professionals is an exciting idea, allowing some of the top players in the world to compete. At the other end of the spectrum, by limiting it to professionals twenty and under, we're following the purest of the Olympic traditions...

"I assume the qualifications will be reassessed between now and 1988. If there's no change, the 1988 Olympics will be the first to allow professionals to compete for medals."

The twenty-and-under provision is a "one-time trial," according to Bob Kramer, executive director of the Southern California Tennis Association, which assisted in the planning of the new UCLA Tennis Center. But Kramer hopes it will serve as a catalyst toward a rethinking of Olympic eligibility requirements.

"I'd like to see tennis used to open things up," Kramer said. "This will be the first time an open competition has been included in the Olympics—at least the first time admitted professionals have been able to compete. The Olympics have always stood for amateur competition, but are the members of the Russian Army hockey team, who stay together for years, really amateur? If the Olympics were open to everyone, there would be less discrimination. If tennis is successful in 1984, maybe a similar concept could be used in the future."

In 1984, the Olympic tennis exhibition will be open to any player born during or after 1964. Among those eligible to participate in the thirty-two-player men's field will be Mats Wilander of Sweden, the 1982 French Open champion; Jimmy Arias of the United States, ranked among the world's top 10; Aaron Krickstein of the U.S., who reached the round of 16 in the 1983 U.S. Open, and Pat Cash of Australia, ranked among the top 40 in the world.

The women's division will be open to such professionals as No. 3-ranked Andrea Jaeger of the U.S., Andrea Temesvari of Hungary, top-20 players Kathy Rinaldi of the U.S. and Carling Bassett of Canada, and top-30 players Kathy Horvath of the U.S. and Helena Sukova of Czechoslovakia.

The system hasn't appeased all observers. At least one top pro, Martina Navratilova, has criticized the age limit as discriminatory. Navratilova turns twenty-eight in 1984.

Most of the field, however, will consist of amateurs. Of the thirty-two players seeded in each division (men's and women's singles), twenty will be selected by the International Tennis Federation from nominations made by national associations, four will be chosen by the United States Tennis Federation and eight will be awarded berths according to their position in the 1983 junior world rankings. With the exception of the U.S., no country will be permitted to enter more than two players in either the men's or women's

brackets. The U.S., as host country, will be allowed four players in each division.

Some countries will hold qualifying tournaments to determine which players will be nominated for Olympic consideration. Others will nominate their top-ranked players. The eight U.S. contestants will be decided after an Olympic trials tournament.

The Olympic competition will last six days, a single-elimination tournament with first-round play starting August 6 and finals for both men and women August 11. Matches will be best-of-three sets, and although no medals will be presented, the top four finishers will receive special awards.

Tennis last appeared in the Olympics in 1968, also as a demonstration, and has not been a medal sport for sixty years. It made its debut along with the modern Olympics in Athens in 1896 and was featured, in some form, in every Olympics through 1924. The finale in 1924 was a memorable one for the U.S., which won gold medals in all five events—men's singles and doubles, women's singles and doubles, and mixed doubles. Helen Wills (women's singles and doubles), Vincent Richards (men's singles and doubles) and Hazel Wightman (women's doubles and mixed doubles) were double winners for the Americans.

Politics within the governing bodies of tennis led to the sport's elimination from the Games after 1924. There was a conflict with Wimbledon over which tournament represented a true world's championship. There was a struggle between the IOC and the Lawn Tennis Association for control of the Olympic sport. And there was the ongoing debate over whether professionals should be allowed to participate in the Olympics.

Tennis's return to the Olympics has been met with enthusiasm by the public. By late October of 1983, all six days of the demonstration had been sold out. "Tennis is a sport Southern California has always enjoyed," Burke said. "For many tennis fans, this is a once-in-a-lifetime opportunity."

Opposite top: *Canada's 16-year-old whiz Carling Bassett, already a seasoned pro, could earn her country Olympic honors. AP Laserphoto*

Opposite bottom: *Ranked sixth in the world early in 1984, New York's Jimmy Arias will be a likely U.S. player if he chooses to forego two weeks of the lucrative pro tour. AP Laserphoto*

Left: *Professionals such as Andrea Jaeger would be eligible to compete under the relaxed rules that will apply in tennis, one of the two demonstration sports at this summer's Olympic Games. The other is baseball. Photo by Ken Hively/Los Angeles Times*

BASEBALL
BY BOB CUOMO

When the first pitch is made to start the Olympic baseball competition the afternoon of July 31 at Dodger Stadium, the happiest and proudest person in the park will be Rod Dedeaux. "The International Olympic Committee's decision to adopt baseball is the culmination of everything I've worked for," said Dedeaux, baseball coach at the University of Southern California and the head coach of the United States entry in the eight-day demonstration tournament. The U.S. will play teams from Cuba, Nicaragua, Italy, South Korea and Taiwan.

Dedeaux's dream would have had an even happier ending if the International Olympic Committee (IOC), meeting in Lausanne, Switzerland, April 9, 1981, had made baseball a medal sport, rather than a demonstration sport. Gaining permanent status for baseball is the ultimate goal of Dedeaux, as well as Dodger President Peter O'Malley, United States Baseball Federation President Robert E. Smith and international amateur baseball officials Bruno Ben-

eck of Italy and Manuel Gonzales Guerra of Cuba.

The drive began early in 1978, when the United States Baseball Federation (USBF) formed a steering committee for the purpose of promoting and expediting the acceptance of baseball as an Olympic sport. The committee was headed by Dedeaux, a longtime advocate of international amateur baseball. The committee's primary task was to generate enthusiasm and get support from the International Association of Amateur Baseball (AINBA). Progress was slow until Smith, as USBF president, became active in the group. He eventually was named its acting president. The turning point came in September, 1979, when Dedeaux and Smith organized a three-day conference for AINBA members in Los Angeles. The conference, hosted by the Dodgers, also was attended by Baseball Commissioner Bowie Kuhn and representatives of the Los Angeles Olympic Organizing Committee (LAOOC). The group was addressed by Kuhn, who pledged major league baseball's support of the movement. O'Malley also spoke to the delegates. Guerra, the head of AINBA's executive council, and other members came away from the conference with a new-found deter-

mination to make baseball part of the Olympics.

But first, an AINBA commission, which included Dedeaux, Smith and Beneck, had to convince the LAOOC that baseball was worthy of being included in the 1984 Games, that it was of general interest and had potential to be financially successful. With assistance from the Dodgers, who helped devise a financial proposal, the AINBA Olympic plan was presented to the LAOOC, which also heard presentations from seven other sports—tennis, softball, roller skating, table tennis, bowling, badminton and orienteering. Each was trying to obtain demonstration status. "We just showed what we can do in attendance," said Dedeaux. "We are totally committed that all eight nights will be sellouts—fifty-five thousand people in Dodger Stadium."

After three months of deliberations, the LAOOC decided to recommend baseball and tennis to the IOC for final approval. And, much to the delight of Dedeaux and the others, the IOC obliged.

Baseball already has been played in the Olympics six times—1904 in St. Louis, 1912 in Stockholm, 1936 in Berlin, 1952 in Helsinki, 1956 in Melbourne and 1964 in Tokyo—but on those occasions

Shane Mack, a UCLA junior who hit .419 last year, is one of the top amateur baseball players in the country and is expected to be in right field for the U.S. in the demonstration tournament during the Olympics. Photo by Jayne Kamin/ Los Angeles Times

two teams played only one exhibition game. This is the first time teams will compete in a tournament format. The six nations will form two divisions of three teams each. Over the first six days of competition, every team will play four games, two within its division and two against teams from the other division. A doubleheader is scheduled each day. Then, ranked by won-lost records, the top team in each division will play the runner-up from the other division in the semifinals. On August 7, the semifinal losers will play for third place and the two winners will meet in the championship game. IOC President Juan Antonio Samaranch will preside at the awards ceremony, and the top three teams will receive specially designed medals.

The United States, as host country for the Games, automatically fields a team. South Korea, by virtue of winning the 1982 world amateur championship, also received an automatic berth. The other teams had to earn their way into the tournament. Italy won the European championship last July; Cuba and Nicaragua finished 1-2 in the Pan American Games in August; Taiwan won the Asian Games in September.

Baseball is America's national pastime, but it is rapidly becoming an international pastime as well. The game is played to some degree in seventy-seven countries. That's more than play many official Olympic sports. AINBA's membership is forty-eight. But just because baseball originated in the United States and Americans have played it longer doesn't necessarily mean that the U.S. has an easy track to the Olympic championship. The favorite probably is Cuba. And the other teams are so strong that the U.S. might not even be among the top three finishers. The U.S. will have the youngest and least-experienced team in the tournament. It will be comprised primarily of college juniors. The Cubans, whose average age is about twenty-eight, have spent many years playing together, dominating international competition. Dedeaux said he's certain that ten or twelve of the Cuban players could play Triple-A or major league ball.

To help the United States field its strongest team, last fall the USBF conducted sixty-five regional tryout camps in hopes of attracting the country's best amateur players. The top player(s) in each camp advanced to a two-day national camp in Louisville, Kentucky, where they were appraised by Dedeaux and his coaching staff. The final twenty-man squad will be announced in June.

Victor Mesa of Cuba does a kung-fu slide at U.S.A. catcher Jim Puzey in a Pan Am final that Cuba won 8-1. The U.S. took bronze. AP Laserphoto

TEAM HANDBALL

BY TOM HAMILTON

Imagine a sport that combines the pace and excitement of basketball, the strategy of soccer and the team play of water polo. Place the sport indoors on a floor about a third larger than a basketball court, with seven players on each team attempting to throw a leather-covered, inflated ball about the size of a cantaloupe into a mesh goal and—presto!—you've got team handball.

Team handball is an Olympic sport clouded in ambiguity and anonymity. Some suggest it is inappropriately named. What is certain is that team handball has many of the prerequisites for popularity in the United States: intense action with lots of scoring. The game is played in thirty-minute halves, with timeouts allowed for injury only. Included on each seven-man team is a goalie who defends a goal mouth roughly 9 feet wide and 6½ feet high. The six field players in front of him are part of his defense. A typical final score is in the twenties, one point per goal. The object is to dribble and/or pass the ball so quickly that the defensive team is out of position and a score is possible by throwing the ball into the goal.

When a team is on defense, the six field players arrange themselves around the goal in a protective semicircle and try to block the ball or knock it out of an opponent's hand. The offense arranges itself in a complementary semicircle much like a basketball team operating a four-corner offense. The ball is designed to be thrown (for passes or shots) with one hand. Dribbling is allowed, but the emphasis is placed on passing with speed and precision. Players may run for three steps with the ball. They may also hold it for three seconds in their hands or on the floor.

Team handball was first introduced as an eleven-man game played outdoors in the 1936 Olympics in Berlin. After World War II, team handball moved indoors and gained prominence with a seven-man version of the original game. It became an official Olympic sport for men in 1972. A women's version was added in 1977. It is a popular sport in Europe. The International Handball Federation has 4.2 million members in eighty countries, but only slightly more than one percent of those live in the U.S. It is estimated that ten thousand Americans have played the game since it was officially organized under the United States Team Handball Federation (USTHF) in 1959.

The sport's supporters are counting on Olympic exposure from the media

and hoping for some timely upsets against the traditionally stronger Eastern Europeans to give the sport a boost in the U.S. "Imagine American football eighty or ninety years ago—that's where we are now," said Mike Cavanaugh, coach of the 1980 Olympic team. "There's no money for the players, no perks, no promises, no fame, no future. Once you're done, you're done. All you get out of it is playing the game."

Obviously, Americans are years behind established team handball powers. The East German men and Soviet Union women won the gold medals in 1980. Members of these teams are veterans of the sport. Some members of the U.S. team handball squads have played the game for as little as two years.

The U.S. national men's team trained at three sites in New Jersey in preparation for the Games; the women trained in Lake Placid, New York. The coaches are Javier Garcia Cuesta, a thirty-six-year-old Spaniard who emigrated to this country in 1979 and will coach the men's team, and Klement Capliar, a forty-two-year-old Czechoslovakian who defected in 1967, has gained Canadian citizenship and will coach the women's team. Cuesta played for Spain's national team for ten years and partici-

pated in the 1972 Olympics in Munich. Capliar, who began to coach the women's team in 1982, estimated that the women's team was ten goals behind the world powers when he took over. But they scored a major upset over powerful Denmark last summer, and Capliar began talking about winning a medal in the Olympics.

Both coaches, while using the same strategy in preparation for the Games—keep it simple—have had to scramble to build their respective programs. Cuesta found athletes from other sports and developed them into team handball players. Goalkeeper Bill Kessler was discovered on Adelphi College's lacrosse team. Rod Ohista is a former UC Irvine water polo player who was added to the national team after performing well in the National Sports Festival. Capliar, while in Colorado Springs for the festival, spent as much time scouting female athletes in other sports as he did watching America's best team handball players. He says that softball and field hockey players can learn the game in a year.

Only a good dose of international competition in the L.A. Olympics will tell just how many fast learners Cuesta and Capliar found.

Team handball, played in the Olympics by both men's and women's teams, has seldom been seen in the U.S., but there are those who say it is an idea whose time has come. Photos by Joe Kennedy/Los Angeles Times

FIELD HOCKEY

BY ALLAN DROOZ

If you or your ancestors ever claimed fealty to the Queen of England you probably know all about field hockey. The rugged outdoor sport that combines the running and agility of soccer with the stick handling and collisions of its spinoff, ice hockey, is relatively unknown in the United States, where it is played on an organized level only by women.

But the fast-paced game, which originated in England and spread throughout the British Empire, is a national craze in India and Pakistan, which have dominated the men's international level since the 1920s. When India beat Great Britain for the Olympic gold medal in 1948 in London, a year after its long-sought independence, it was cause for national celebration. It was hardly unexpected, though, since India had won every gold medal since 1928. India continued the streak through 1960, when bitter rival Pakistan beat India in the final. India and Pakistan remain the men's teams to beat in 1984, with top competition expected from West Germany, Australia, New Zealand, Holland and England. India is the defending men's champion.

The U.S. men, making their first Olympic appearance since 1956, are an underdog team, though they have been rising steadily under Coach Gavin Featherstone, a former British Olympian. Featherstone, who has been directing the team since 1982, is hoping to establish the U.S. as a strong team in 1984 and a gold medal contender in 1988. Since field hockey is not a men's collegiate sport in the U.S., Featherstone has recruited athletes from other sports. Up-and-coming players Drew Stone and goalie Bob Stiles were convinced to switch over from basketball and football. Featherstone has also been developing a national youth program, which has already produced two promising teen-agers, Mohammad Barakat and Alvin Pagan. Barakat will be on the Olympic team at age seventeen.

The game was introduced in the United States as a genteel ladies' sport, played in skirts and white blouses, and is the oldest women's team sport in the U.S. It remains a popular women's sport around the world—including the East Coast of the U.S., where it may no longer be all that genteel. The middle of a scrambling pack of players slashing with sticks at a leather ball is no place for the squeamish—or anyone worried about keeping attractive shins.

European countries such as Holland and England, and former British outposts such as Australia and New Zealand, are the world powers among the women, but North America is gaining fast. Canada, which finished second in the 1983 World Cup, and the U.S. expect to be fighting for a medal in Los Angeles. Holland, which boasts the world's top penalty corner shooter in Fieke Boekhorst, won the 1983 World Cup. Zimbabwe is the defending Olympic gold medalist but is not among the 1984 favorites, many of whom boycotted Moscow in 1980.

The U.S. women, under Coach Vonnie Gros, have several players, notably Beth Anders, who have been training with the team for a decade. Anders, considered one of the world's best penalty corner shooters, is a successful collegiate coach at Old Dominion University. Gros (pronounced grow) was a multiple-sport athlete in the South Jersey–Philadelphia area in the early 1950s and coached West Chester (Pennsylvania) State College to two national titles in the mid-1970s before taking over the national team. Gros's veteran 1984 team will have twelve members of the 1980 Olympic team, including Anders and 1980 captain Julie Staver, a veteran of three World Cups.

The sport is played on a 100-by-60-yard field, and the rules are similar to soccer: eleven-member teams including goalie play thirty-five-minute halves. The ball, slightly larger than a baseball, is wrapped in either leather or plastic and is struck with a wooden stick whose curved shooting end is some-

what smaller than in ice hockey. The ball can be shot only in a 16-yard semi-circle around the 4-yard-wide, 7-foot-high goal. The ball cannot be advanced with the hands or feet except by the goalkeeper. The ball can be caught by players if dropped immediately into play. The stick cannot be used to obstruct opponents and cannot be carried higher than the shoulders. Penalties within the shooting area or personal fouls within 25 yards of the end line result in a corner penalty shot. Most of the game's points are scored on corner penalty shots. On a penalty corner, a player on the attacking team gets the ball 10 yards from the net. No defender is allowed in the attacking circle until the ball is put in play. Then the defense may rush the shooter, who by that time usually has taken a clear shot. Most teams usually have a player who takes most of the penalty corner shots.

There is evidence of predecessors to the modern game dating back to ancient Egypt, Greece and Persia. Drawings show similar stick-and-ball games. The rough Persian version reportedly accounted for several deaths. The first official men's team was founded in England in 1860. English troops introduced the game in India, where the natives evolved a style that combined extraordinary stick-handling finesse with great stamina.

The Indians developed a dynasty behind Dhyan Chand, that nation's Babe Ruth. In Chand's ten years as the team's star (1926–36), the Indians won all three Olympic gold medals and out-scored opponents 102-3. During a 1935 tour of New Zealand, Chand scored 201 of the two teams' 584 goals. In the 1972 Olympics at Munich, West Germany finally broke the Indian subcontinent's gold stranglehold, introducing a man-to-man style defense to defeat Pakistan, 10-0, in the final. Pakistan's somewhat surly acceptance of that defeat earned the Pakistani field hockey federation a suspension. India and Pakistan's approach to 1984 figures to be no less intense.

The field of play in Los Angeles will be an artificial surface at East Los Angeles College. Twelve men's and six women's teams will be split into two pools, with the top teams in round-robin play advancing to semifinals.

U.S. goalie Jon O'Haire blocks a shot by Argentina in the 1983 Pan Am Games. Argentina won 4-0 but lost the gold medal to Canada. AP Laserphoto

SOCCER

BY GRAHAME JONES

It was not all that long ago that soccer in the Olympic Games was taken seriously. Very seriously.

Consider 1920, for instance. That was the year the Czechoslovakian team stormed off the field in the championship game, allowing Belgium, which was leading 2-0 at the time, to win the gold medal. The Czechs were unhappy with the officiating at Antwerp.

Then there was 1936, when it was the fans' turn to storm onto the field in Berlin. Peru was playing Austria and the game was tied in overtime, 2-2. A small group of Peruvian fans staged a mini-riot, Peru scored twice during the melee and "won," 4-2. A replay was ordered, Peru failed to show up and Austria went on to win the silver medal.

Olympic soccer still is taken seriously, but not by the major soccer-playing nations of Western Europe and South America. They prefer to concentrate their efforts on the World Cup, which means most of the medals have been heading Eastern Europe's way for the past three decades.

When Hungary won the gold at Helsinki in 1952, it began a streak that remains unbroken. The Hungarians have won two more gold medals since then, while the Soviet Union, Yugoslavia, Poland, East Germany and Czechoslovakia have each won one. In fact, of the twenty-four medals awarded since 1952—gold, silver and bronze— all but four have gone to Eastern European nations. Denmark managed to grab a silver in 1968. Sweden, Italy and Japan have each earned a bronze.

There is no reason to believe that things will be any different in 1984. Almost one hundred nations entered teams in the year-long Olympic qualifying tournaments that took place worldwide. Only fourteen will make it to Los Angeles, joining the United States, which automatically qualifies as the host nation, and Czechoslovakia, the defending champion.

Eastern Europe's dominance should continue. The Czechs won in Moscow in 1980 by defeating East Germany, while the Soviet Union won the bronze by beating Yugoslavia. The same quartet could well make the final four this year, too.

As for the United States, it is pleased merely to be assured a place in the final

sixteen. The U.S. has entered every Olympic soccer tournament since 1924, but even when it has gained a spot in the Olympics, it has not done well. For example, Argentina scored an 11-2 victory over the Americans in 1928 and Italy beat the U.S. in 1948, 9-0, and in 1952, 8-0.

Those lopsided scores are unlikely to be repeated in 1984, but end results should be the same. The U.S. team, made up of collegiate players and players from the North American Soccer League and the Major Indoor Soccer League playing on amateur contracts, has been preparing by participating in tournaments and exhibitions in such places as South Korea, Malaysia and Honduras. The opposition it will face in the Olympics will be far tougher, however, so a first-round exit is expected. For the U.S. to qualify for the quarter-finals would be a major upset.

No matter who qualifies, soccer may surprise many by the size of its crowds. More than ten months before the first ball is kicked, the championship match August 11 in the 104,696-seat Rose Bowl had been sold out. In all, a half-million tickets had been ordered for the soccer tournament, which will be held at four spacious sites—the Rose Bowl

Rodriguez of Cuba battles American Tim Schultz for possession in Caracas, Venezuela. AP Laserphoto

in Pasadena, Stanford University, the Naval Academy at Annapolis and Harvard University.

Soccer traditionally has been among the most popular of the Olympic sports, outdistancing track and field, boxing, swimming and basketball in terms of attendance. In Moscow in 1980, the sport attracted a total of 1,821,624 fans, accounting for 35.48 percent of all tickets sold. In Montreal four years earlier, 647,683 fans passed through the turnstiles, this despite the fact that Canada is not a major soccer-playing nation. The championship game that year between East Germany and Poland drew 71,619 fans to the Olympic Stadium, the largest crowd ever to see a sporting event in Canada.

The history of soccer is replete with the names of players who first appeared on their country's Olympic team and then became international celebrities—players such as Brazil's Junior, Poland's Kazimierz Deyna, France's Michel Platini, the Soviet Union's Oleg Blokhin and Mexico's Hugo Sanchez.

The same sort of emergence of a new generation of stars, players who will go on to World Cup fame in Mexico in 1986, is likely in Los Angeles. And the sport they will be showcasing is one that has captivated millions of fans for more than a century. Soccer, when played as it should be played, is, as its greatest practitioner, Pele, once put it, "the beautiful game."

Visually, it provides scenes such as the spectacular flying save of a goalkeeper stretched full length to claw the ball out of the air, the overhead bicycle kick made famous by the talented Brazilians, the crunching desperation of a sliding tackle, the power of a shot hammered toward the goal from 30 yards.

And, although soccer is certainly a contact sport, there is also a stress on finesse. Players must know how to trap the ball with their chest, thigh or foot to bring it instantly under control. They must know how to dribble past opponents by using feints, changes of pace and high-speed footwork that would impress a top-flight boxer. They must know how to run intelligently off the ball, to position themselves in the most advantageous way to aid their own team or thwart the opponent. Precise cross-field passes or cheeky backheels to a teammate must become second nature. Heading the ball well is an art in itself.

To those unfamiliar with the sport, the ever-changing pattern of players on the field looks like mass confusion. But it is this very fluidity, this kaleidoscope of action, that gives soccer an unpredictability and a special appeal. Coaching is done before the game begins. Once on the field, players are on their own during the 90-minute duration of the game. Two 45-minute halves with no timeouts mean the action is virtually nonstop. Players can run as much as five to seven miles in a game.

The creative skill and the freedom of expression shown by such players as Johann Cruyff, for example, give the world's game its unique flavor. The most soccer fans can hope for in Los Angeles in 1984 is that another Pele, Best or Cruyff will make his appearance. Even if he does take the gold medal back to Eastern Europe.

Michael Fox (left) of the U.S.A. heads a ball away from a Chilean halfback in Pan Am Games action. Uruguay took top honors. AP Laserphoto

OLYMPIC GOLD MEDAL WINNERS OF 1976, 1980 AND 1984

BY MIKE KENNEDY

ARCHERY

MEN
1976
| Darrell Pace | United States | 2,571 |
1980
| Tomi Poikolainen | Finland | 2,455 |
1984

WOMEN
1976
| Luann Ryon | United States | 2,499 |
1980
| Keto Losaberidze | USSR | 2,491 |
1984

BASKETBALL

MEN
1976
United States
1980
Yugoslavia
1984

WOMEN
1976
USSR
1980
USSR
1984

BOXING

LIGHT-FLYWEIGHT (106 lbs.)
1976
| Jorge Hernandez | Cuba |
1980
| Shamil Sabyrov | USSR |
1984

FLYWEIGHT (112.5 lbs.)
1976
| Leo Randolph | United States |
1980
| Petar Lessov | Bulgaria |
1984

BANTAMWEIGHT (119 lbs.)
1976
| Yong Jo Gu | North Korea |
1980
| Juan Hernandez | Cuba |
1984

FEATHERWEIGHT (126 lbs.)
1976
| Angel Herrera | Cuba |
1980
| Rudi Fink | East Germany |
1984

LIGHTWEIGHT (132 lbs.)
1976
| Howard Davis | United States |
1980
| Angel Herrera | Cuba |
1984

LIGHT-WELTERWEIGHT (140 lbs.)
1976
| Ray Leonard | United States |
1980
| Patrizio Oliva | Italy |
1984

WELTERWEIGHT (148 lbs.)
1976
| Jochen Bachfeld | East Germany |
1980
| Andres Aldama | Cuba |
1984

LIGHT-MIDDLEWEIGHT (157 lbs.)
1976
| Jerzy Rybicki | Poland |
1980
| Armando Martinez | Cuba |
1984

MIDDLEWEIGHT (165 lbs.)
1976
| Michael Spinks | United States |
1980
| Jose Gomez | Cuba |
1984

LIGHT-HEAVYWEIGHT (179 lbs.)
1976
| Leon Spinks | United States |
1980
| Slobodan Kacar | Yugoslavia |
1984

HEAVYWEIGHT (200 lbs.)
1976
| Teofilo Stevenson | Cuba |
1980
| Teofilo Stevenson | Cuba |
1984

CANOEING

MEN

KAYAK SINGLES (500 Meters)
1976
| Vasile Diba | Romania | 1:46.41 |
1980
| Vladimir Parfenovich | USSR | 1:43.43 |
1984

KAYAK SINGLES (1,000 Meters)
1976
| Rudiger Helm | East Germany | 3:48.20 |
1980
| Rudiger Helm | East Germany | 3:48.77 |
1984

KAYAK PAIRS (500 Meters)
1976
| J. Mattern-B. Olbricht | East Germany | 1:35.87 |
1980
| V. Parfenovich-S. Chukhrai | USSR | 1:32.38 |
1984

KAYAK PAIRS (1,000 Meters)
1976
| S. Nagorny-V. Romanovsky | USSR | 3:29.01 |
1980
| V. Parfenovich-S. Chukhrai | USSR | 3:26.72 |
1984

KAYAK FOURS (1,000 Meters)
1976
| S. Chukhrai-A. Degtiarev-Y. Filatov-V. Morozof | USSR | 3:08.69 |
1980
| B. Olbricht-B. Duvigneau-R. Helm-H. Marg | East Germany | 3:13.76 |
1984

CANADIAN SINGLES (500 Meters)
1976
| Aleksandr Rogov | USSR | 1:59.23 |
1980
| Sergei Postrekhin | USSR | 1:53.37 |
1984

CANADIAN SINGLES (1,000 Meters)
1976
| Matija Ljubek | Yugoslavia | 4:09.51 |
1980
| Lubomir Lyubenov | Bulgaria | 4:12.38 |
1984

CANADIAN PAIRS (500 Meters)
1976
| S. Petrenko-A. Vinogradov | USSR | 1:45.81 |
1980
| L. Foltan-I. Vaskuti | Hungary | 1:43.39 |
1984

CANADIAN PAIRS (1,000 Meters)
1976
S. Petrenko-
  A. Vinogradov   USSR   3:52.76
1980
I. Patzaichin-
  T. Simionov   Romania   3:47.65
1984

WOMEN
KAYAK SINGLES (500 Meters)
1976
Carola Zirzov   East Germany   2:01.05
1980
Birgit Fischer   East Germany   1:57.96
1984

KAYAK PAIRS (500 Meters)
1976
N. Gopova-G. Kreft   USSR   1:51.15
1980
C. Genauss-
  M. Bischof   East Germany   1:43.88
1984

CYCLING
1,000-METER SPRINT
1976
Anton Tkac   Czechoslovakia   10.78
1980
Lutz Hesslich   East Germany   11.40
1984

1,000-METER TIME TRIAL
1976
Klaus-Jurgen Grunke   West Germany   1:05.927
1980
Lothar Thoms   East Germany   1:02.955
1984

4,000-METER INDIVIDUAL PURSUIT
1976
Gregor Braun   East Germany   4:47.61
1980
Robert Dill-Bundi   Switzerland   4:35.66
1984

4,000-METER TEAM PURSUIT
1976
G. Braun-H. Lutz-
  G. Schumacher-
  P. Vonhof   West Germany   4:21.06
1980
V. Manakov-
  V. Movchan-
  V. Osokin-
  V. Petrakov   USSR   4:15.70
1984

INDIVIDUAL ROAD RACE
1976
Bernt Johansson   Sweden   4:46:52
1980
Sergei
  Sukhoruchenkov   USSR   4:48:28
1984

ROAD RACE TIME TRIAL
1976
A. Chukanov-
  V. Chaplygin-
  V. Kaminsky-
  A. Pikkuus   USSR   2:08:53

1980
Y. Kashirin-O. Logvin-
  S. Shelpakov-
  A. Yarkin   USSR   2:01:21.7
1984

EQUESTRIAN
GRAND PRIX JUMPING (Individual)
1976
Alwin Schockmohle   West Germany   0
1980
Jan Kowalczyk   Poland   8
1984

GRAND PRIX JUMPING (Team)
1976
H. Parot-M. Rozier-
  M. Roche-
  M. Roquet   France   40
1980
V. Chukanov-
  V. Poganovsky-
  V. Asmayev-
  N. Korolkov   USSR   20¼
1984

GRAND PRIX DRESSAGE (Individual)
1976
Christine
  Stuckelberger   Switzerland   1,486
1980
Elizabeth Theurer   Austria   1,370
1984

GRAND PRIX DRESSAGE (Team)
1976
H. Boldt-R. Klimke-
  G. Grillo   West Germany   5,155
1980
Y. Kovshov-
  V. Ugryumov-
  V. Misevich   USSR   4,383
1984

THREE-DAY EVENT (Individual)
1976
Edmund Coffin   United States   114.99
1980
Euro Federico Ramon   Italy   108.6
1984

THREE-DAY EVENT (Team)
1976
E. Coffin-J. Plumb-
  B. Davidson   United States   441.00
1980
A. Blinov-Y. Salnikov-
  V. Volkov   USSR   457.00
1984

FENCING
MEN
FOIL (Individual)
1976
Fabio Dal Zotto   Italy
1980
Vladimir Smirnov   USSR
1984

FOIL (Team)
1976
M. Behr-T. Bach-

H. Hein-
  K. Reichert   West Germany
1980
D. Flament-P. Jolyot-
  B. Boscherie-
  P. Bonnin   France
1984

EPEE (Individual)
1976
Alexander Pusch   West Germany
1980
Johan Harmenberg   Sweden
1984

EPEE (Team)
1976
C. Von Essen-
  H. Jacobson-
  L. Hogstrom-
  R. Edling   Sweden
1980
P. Riboud-P. Picot-
  H. Gardas-
  P. Boisse   France
1984

SABRE (Individual)
1976
Viktor Krovopuskov   USSR
1980
Viktor Krovopuskov   USSR
1984

SABRE (Team)
1976
V. Krovopuskov-
  E. Vinokurov-
  V. Sidiak-
  V. Nazlymov   USSR
1980
M. Burtsev-
  V. Krovopuskov-
  V. Sidiak-
  V. Nazlymov   USSR
1984

WOMEN
FOIL (Individual)
1976
Ildiko
  Schwarczenberger   Hungary
1980
Pascale Trinquet   France
1984

FOIL (Team)
1976
E. Belova-V. Sidorova-
  O. Kniazeva-
  N. Guilanova   USSR
1980
B. Gaudin-
  P. Trinquet-
  I. Boeri-Begard-
  V. Brouquier   France
1984

GYMNASTICS
MEN
1976
TEAM
H. Igarashi-
  S. Fujimoto-S. Kato-
  H. Kajiyama-

E. Kenmotsu- M. Tsukahara	Japan	576.85

ALL-AROUND
Nikolai Andrianov	USSR	116.650

FLOOR EXERCISE
Nikolai Andrianov	USSR	19.450

POMMEL HORSE
Zoltan Magyar	Hungary	19.700

RINGS
Nikolai Andrianov	USSR	19.650

VAULT
Nikolai Andrianov	USSR	19.450

PARALLEL BARS
Sawao Kato	Japan	19.675

HORIZONTAL BAR
Mitsuo Tsukahara	Japan	19.675

1980

TEAM
N. Andrianov- A. Ditiatin- E. Asaryan- A. Tkachyov- B. Makuts- V. Markelov	USSR	589.60

ALL-AROUND
Alexandr Ditiatin	USSR	118.650

FLOOR EXERCISE
Roland Bruckner	East Germany	19.750

POMMEL HORSE
Zoltan Magyar	Hungary	19.925

RINGS
Alexandr Ditiatin	USSR	19.875

VAULT
Nikolai Andrianov	USSR	19.825

PARALLEL BARS
Alexandr Tkachyov	USSR	19.775

HORIZONTAL BAR
Stoyan Deltchev	Bulgaria	19.825

1984

TEAM

ALL-AROUND

FLOOR EXERCISE

POMMEL HORSE

RINGS

VAULT

PARALLEL BARS

HORIZONTAL BAR

WOMEN

1976

TEAM
S. Grozdova-E. Saadi- M. Filatova- O. Korbut- L. Tourischeva- N. Kim	USSR	466.00

ALL-AROUND
Nadia Comaneci	Romania	79.275

VAULT
Nelli Kim	USSR	19.800

UNEVEN PARALLEL BARS
Nadia Comaneci	Romania	20.000

BALANCE BEAM
Nadia Comaneci	Romania	19.800

FLOOR EXERCISE
Nelli Kim	USSR	19.850

1980

TEAM
N. Shaposhnikova- Y. Davidova-N. Kim- M. Filatova- S. Zacharova- Y. Naimuschina	USSR	394.90

ALL-AROUND
Yelena Davidova	USSR	79.150

VAULT
Natalya Shaposhnikova	USSR	19.725

UNEVEN PARALLEL BARS
Maxi Gnauck	East Germany	19.875

BALANCE BEAM
Nadia Comaneci	Romania	19.800

FLOOR EXERCISE
(tie) Nelli Kim	USSR	19.875
(tie) Nadia Comaneci	Romania	19.875

1984

TEAM

ALL-AROUND

VAULT

UNEVEN PARALLEL BARS

BALANCE BEAM

FLOOR EXERCISE

RHYTHMIC GYMNASTICS

TEAM HANDBALL
MEN
1976
USSR
1980
East Germany
1984

WOMEN
1976
USSR
1980
USSR
1984

FIELD HOCKEY
MEN
1976
New Zealand
1980
India
1984

WOMEN
1976
Event not held
1980
Zimbabwe
1984

JUDO
BANTAMWEIGHT (132 lbs.)
1976
Event not held
1980
Thierry Rey	France
1984

FEATHERWEIGHT (143 lbs.)
1976
Event not held
1980
Nikolai Solodukhin	USSR
1984

LIGHTWEIGHT (156½ lbs.)
1976
Hector Rodriguez	Cuba
1980
Ezio Gamba	Italy
1984

LIGHT MIDDLEWEIGHT (172 lbs.)
1976
Vladimir Nevzorov	USSR
1980
Shota Khabareli	USSR
1984

MIDDLEWEIGHT (189½ lbs.)
1976
Isamu Sonoda	Japan
1980
Juerg Roethlisberger	Switzerland
1984

LIGHT HEAVYWEIGHT (209 lbs.)
1976
Kazuhiro Ninomiya	Japan
1980
Robert Van De Walle	Belgium
1984

HEAVYWEIGHT (Over 209 lbs.)
1976
Sergei Novikov	USSR
1980
Angelo Parisi	France
1984

OPEN
1976
Haruki Uemura	Japan
1980
Dietmar Lorenz	East Germany
1984

MODERN PENTATHLON
INDIVIDUAL
1976
Janusz Pyciak-Peciak	Poland	5,520
1980
Anatoly Starostin	USSR	5,568
1984

TEAM
1976
A. Parker- R. Nightingale- J. Fox	Britain	15,559
1980
A. Starostin-P. Lednev- Y. Lipeyev	USSR	16,126
1984

ROWING

SINGLE SCULLS
1976
Pertti Karppinen | Finland | 7:29.03
1980
Pertti Karppinen | Finland | 7:09.61
1984

DOUBLE SCULLS
1976
F. Hansen-A. Hansen | Norway | 7:13.20
1980
J. Dreifke-
K. Kroppelien | East Germany | 6:24.33
1984

QUADRUPLE SCULLS
1976
W. Guldenpfenning-
R. Reiche-
K. Bussert-
M. Wolfgramm | East Germany | 6:18.65
1980
F. Dundr-K. Bunk-
U. Heppner-
M. Winter | East Germany | 5:49.81
1984

COXLESS PAIRS
1976
J. Landvoigt-
B. Landvoigt | East Germany | 7:23.31
1980
J. Landvoigt-
B. Landvoigt | East Germany | 6:48.01
1984

COXED PAIRS
1976
H. Jarling-F. Ulrich-
G. Spohr (cox) | East Germany | 7:58.99
1980
H. Jarling-R. Ulrick-
G. Spohr (cox) | East Germany | 7:02.54
1984

COXLESS FOURS
1976
S. Brietzke-A. Decker-
S. Semmler-
W. Mager | East Germany | 6:37.42
1980
J. Thiele-A. Decker-
S. Semmler-
S. Brietzke | East Germany | 6:08.17
1984

COXED FOURS
1976
USSR | 6:40.22
1980
East Germany | 6:14.51
1984

EIGHTS
1976
East Germany | 5:58.29
1980
East Germany | 5:49.05
1984

WOMEN
SINGLE SCULLS
1976
Christine Scheiblich | East Germany | 4:05.56
1980
Sanda Toma | Romania | 3:40.69
1984

DOUBLE SCULLS
1976
S. Otzetova-
Z. Yordonova | USSR | 3:44.36
1980
E. Kholptseva-
L. Popova | USSR | 3:16.27
1984

COXLESS PAIRS
1976
S. Barboulova-
S. Kourbatova | Bulgaria | 4:01.22
1980
U. Steindorf-C. Klier | East Germany | 3:30.49
1984

COXED QUADRUPLE SCULLS
1976
East Germany | 3:29.99
1980
East Germany | 3:15.32
1984

COXED FOURS
1976
East Germany | 3:45.08
1980
East Germany | 3:19.27
1984

EIGHTS
1976
East Germany | 3:33.32
1980
East Germany | 3:03.32
1984

SHOOTING

FREE PISTOL (50 Meters)
1976
Uwe Potteck | East Germany | 573
1980
Aleksandr Melentev | USSR | 581
1984

SMALL-BORE RIFLE (Prone Position)
1976
Karlheintz Smieszek | West Germany | 599
1980
Karoly Varga | Hungary | 599
1984

SMALL-BORE RIFLE (Three Positions)
1976
Lanny Bassham | United States | 1,162
1980
Viktor Vlasov | USSR | 1,173
1984

RAPID-FIRE PISTOL
1976
Norbert Klaar | East Germany | 597
1980
Corneliu Ion | Romania | 596
1984

OLYMPIC TRAP SHOOTING
1976
Donald Haldeman | United States | 190
1980
Luciano Giovannetti | Italy | 198
1984

SKEET SHOOTING
1976
Josef Panacek | Czechoslovakia | 198
1980
Hans Kjeld
Rusmussen | Denmark | 196
1984

RUNNING GAME TARGET
1976
Alexandr Gazov | USSR | 579
1980
Igor Sokolov | USSR | 589
1984

SOCCER
1976
East Germany
1980
Czechoslovakia
1984

SWIMMING
MEN
100-METER FREESTYLE
1976
Jim Montgomery | United States | 49.99
1980
Jorg Woithe | East Germany | 50.40
1984

200-METER FREESTYLE
1976
Bruce Furniss | United States | 1:50.29
1980
Sergei Kopliakov | USSR | 1:49.81
1984

400-METER FREESTYLE
1976
Brian Goodell | United States | 3:51.93
1980
Vladimir Salnikov | USSR | 3:51.31
1984

1,500-METER FREESTYLE
1976
Brian Goodell | United States | 15:02.40
1980
Vladimir Salnikov | USSR | 14:58.27
1984

100-METER BACKSTROKE
1976
John Nabor | United States | 55.49
1980
Bengt Baron | Sweden | 56.31
1984

200-METER BACKSTROKE
1976
John Nabor | United States | 1:59.19

1980

Sandor Wladar — Hungary — 2:01.93

1984

100-METER BREASTSTROKE
1976
John Hencken — United States — 1:03.11
1980
Duncan Goodhew — Britain — 1:03.34
1984

200-METER BREASTSTROKE
1976
David Wilkie — Britain — 2:15.11
1980
Robertas Zhulpa — USSR — 2:15.85
1984

100-METER BUTTERFLY
1976
Matt Vogel — United States — 54.35
1980
Par Arvidsson — Sweden — 54.92
1984

200-METER BUTTERFLY
1976
Michael Bruner — United States — 1:59.23
1980
Sergei Fesenko — USSR — 1:59.76
1984

400-METER INDIVIDUAL MEDLEY
1976
Rod Strachan — United States — 4:23.68
1980
Aleksandr Sidorenko — USSR — 4:22.89
1984

4x100-METER MEDLEY RELAY
1976
J. Nabor-J. Hencken-
M. Vogel-
J. Montgomery — United States — 3:42.22
1980
M. Kerry-P. Evans-
M. Tonelli-
N. Brooks — Australia — 3:45.70
1984

4x200-METER FREESTYLE RELAY
1976
M. Bruner-B. Furniss-
J. Nabor-
J. Montgomery — United States — 7:23.22
1980
S. Kopliakov-
V. Salnikov-
I. Stukolkin-
A. Krylov — USSR — 7:23.50
1984

WOMEN
100-METER FREESTYLE
1976
Kornelia Ender — East Germany — 55.65
1980
Barbara Krause — East Germany — 54.78
1984

200-METER FREESTYLE
1976
Kornelia Ender — East Germany — 1:59.26

1980
Barbara Krause — East Germany — 1:58.33
1984

400-METER FREESTYLE
1976
Petra Thumer — East Germany — 4:09.89
1980
Ines Diers — East Germany — 4:08.76
1984

800-METER FREESTYLE
1976
Petra Thumer — East Germany — 8:37.14
1980
Michelle Ford — Australia — 8:29.90
1984

100-METER BACKSTROKE
1976
Ulrike Richter — East Germany — 1:01.83
1980
Rica Reinisch — East Germany — 1:00.86
1984

200-METER BACKSTROKE
1976
Ulrike Richter — East Germany — 2:13.43
1980
Rica Reinisch — East Germany — 2:11.77
1984

100-METER BREASTSTROKE
1976
Hannelore Anke — East Germany — 1:11.16
1980
Ute Geweniger — East Germany — 1:10.22
1984

200-METER BREASTSTROKE
1976
Marina Koshevaia — USSR — 2:33.35
1980
Lina Kachushite — USSR — 2:29.54
1984

100-METER BUTTERFLY
1976
Kornelia Ender — East Germany — 1:00.13
1980
Caren Matschuck — East Germany — 1:00.42
1984

200-METER BUTTERFLY
1976
Andrea Pollack — East Germany — 2:11.41
1980
Ines Geissler — East Germany — 2:10.44
1984

400-METER INDIVIDUAL MEDLEY
1976
Ulrike Tauber — East Germany — 4:42.77
1980
Petra Schneider — East Germany — 4:36.29
1984

4x100-METER FREESTYLE RELAY
1976
K. Peyton-W. Boglioli-
J. Sterkel-
S. Babashoff — United States — 3:44.82

1980
B. Krause-
C. Metschuck-
I. Diers-
S. Hulsenbeck — East Germany — 3:42.71
1984

4x100-METER MEDLEY RELAY
1976
U. Richter-H. Anke-
A. Pollack-K. Ender — East Germany — 4:07.95
1980
R. Reinisch-
U. Geweniger-
A. Pollack-
C. Metschuck — East Germany — 4:06.67
1984

DIVING
MEN
SPRINGBOARD
1976
Philip Boggs — United States — 619.050
1980
Aleksandr Portnov — USSR — 905.025
1984

PLATFORM
1976
Klaus Dibiasi — Italy — 600.51
1980
Falk Hoffmann — East Germany — 835.650
1984

WOMEN
SPRINGBOARD
1976
Jennifer Chandler — United States — 506.19
1980
Irina Kalinina — USSR — 725.910
1984

PLATFORM
1976
Elena Viatsekhovskaya — USSR — 406.590
1980
Martina Jaschke — East Germany — 596.250
1984

WATER POLO
1976
Hungary
1980
USSR
1984

TRACK AND FIELD
MEN
100 METERS
1976
Hasely Crawford — Trinidad — 10.06
1980
Allan Wells — Britain — 10.25
1984

200 METERS
1976
Don Quarrie — Jamaica — 20.23
1980
Pietro Mennea — Italy — 20.19
1984

400 METERS
1976
Alberto Juantorena Cuba 44.26
1980
Viktor Markin USSR 44.60
1984

800 METERS
1976
Alberto Juantorena Cuba 1:43.5
1980
Steve Ovett Britain 1:45.4
1984

1,500 METERS
1976
John Walker New Zealand 3:39.2
1980
Sebastian Coe Britain 3:38.4
1984

5,000 METERS
1976
Lasse Viren Finland 13:24.8
1980
Miruts Yifter Ethiopia 13:21.0
1984

10,000 METERS
1976
Lasse Viren Finland 27:40.4
1980
Miruts Yifter Ethiopia 27:42.7
1984

MARATHON
1976
Waldemar Cierpinski East Germany 2:09:55
1980
Waldemar Cierpinski East Germany 2:11:03
1984

110-METER HURDLES
1976
Guy Drut France 13.30
1980
Thomas Munkelt East Germany 13.39
1984

400-METER HURDLES
1976
Edwin Moses United States 47.64
1980
Volker Beck East Germany 48.70
1984

3,000-METER STEEPLECHASE
1976
Andres Garderud Sweden 8:08.0
1980
Bronislaw Malinowski Poland 8:09.7
1984

4x100-METER RELAY
1976
H. Glance-J. Jones-
M. Hampton-
S. Riddick United States 38.33
1980
V. Muravyov-
N. Sidorov-
A. Aksinin-
A. Prokofiev USSR 38.26
1984

4x400-METER RELAY
1976
H. Frazier-B. Brown-
F. Newhouse-
M. Parks United States 2:58.7
1980
R. Valyulis-M. Linge-
N. Chernyetsky-
V. Markin USSR 3:01.1
1984

20-KILOMETER WALK
1976
Daniel Bautista Mexico 1:24:40
1980
Maurizio Damilano Italy 1:23:35
1984

50-KILOMETER WALK
1976
Event not held
1980
Hartwig Gauder East Germany 3:49:24
1984

HIGH JUMP
1976
Jacek Wszola Poland 7-4½
1980
Gerd Wessig East Germany 7-8½
1984

POLE VAULT
1976
Tadeusz Slusarski Poland 18-0½
1980
Wladimir Poland 18-11½
  Kozakiewicz
1984

LONG JUMP
1976
Arnie Robinson United States 27-4¾
1980
Lutz Dombrowski East Germany 28-0¼
1984

TRIPLE JUMP
1976
Viktor Saneyev USSR 56-8¾
1980
Jaak Uudmae USSR 56-11¼
1984

SHOT PUT
1976
Udo Beyer East Germany 69-0¾
1980
Vladimir Kiselyov USSR 70-0½
1984

DISCUS
1976
Mac Wilkins United States 221-5
1980
Viktor Rashchupkin USSR 218-8
1984

HAMMER
1976
Yuri Sedykh USSR 254-4
1980
Yuri Sedykh USSR 268-4
1984

JAVELIN
1976
Miklos Nemeth Hungary 310-4
1980
Dainis Kula USSR 299-2
1984

DECATHLON
1976
Bruce Jenner United States 8,618
1980
Daley Thompson Britain 8,495
1984

WOMEN
100 METERS
1976
Annegret Richter West Germany 11.08
1980
Lyudmila Kondratyeva USSR 11.06
1984

200 METERS
1976
Barbel Wockel East Germany 22.37
1980
Barbel Wockel East Germany 22.03
1984

400 METERS
1976
Irena Szewinska Poland 49.29
1980
Marita Koch East Germany 48.88
1984

800 METERS
1976
Tatyana Kazankina USSR 1:54.9
1980
Nadezhda Olizarenko USSR 1:53.5
1984

1,500 METERS
1976
Tatyana Kazankina USSR 4:05.5
1980
Tatyana Kazankina USSR 3:56.6
1984

100-METER HURDLES
1976
Johanna Klier East Germany 12.77
1980
Vera Komisova USSR 12.56
1984

4x100-METER RELAY
1976
M. Gohr-R. Stecher-
C. Bodendorf-
B. Wockel East Germany 42.55
1980
R. Muller-B. Wockel-
I. Auerswald-
M. Gohr East Germany 41.60
1984

4x400-METER RELAY
1976
D. Maletzki-B. Rohde-
E. Streidt-
C. Lathan East Germany 3:19.2

1980
T. Prorochenko-
T. Goichik-
N. Zuskova-
I. Nazarova USSR 3:20.2
1984

MARATHON
1976
Event not held
1980
Event not held
1984

HIGH JUMP
1976
Rosemarie Ackermann East Germany 6-4
1980
Sara Simeoni Italy 6-5½
1984

LONG JUMP
1976
Angela Voigt East Germany 22-0¾
1980
Tatiana Kolpakova USSR 23-2
1984

SHOT PUT
1976
Ivanka Christov Bulgaria 69-5¼
1980
Ilona Slupianek East Germany 73-6¼
1984

DISCUS
1976
Evelin Jahl East Germany 226-4
1980
Evelin Jahl East Germany 229-6
1984

JAVELIN
1976
Ruth Fuchs East Germany 216-4
1980
Maria Colon Cuba 224-5
1984

VOLLEYBALL
MEN
1976
Poland
1980
USSR
1984

WOMEN
1976
Japan
1980
USSR
1984

WEIGHTLIFTING
FLYWEIGHT (114.61 lbs.)
1976
Aleksandr Voronin USSR 534.75
1980
Kanybek Osmanoliev USSR 540
1984

BANTAMWEIGHT (123 lbs.)
1976
Norair Nurikian Bulgaria 578.5
1980
Daniel Nunez Cuba 606.25
1984

FEATHERWEIGHT (132 lbs.)
1976
Nikoilai Kolesnikov USSR 628.25
1980
Viktor Mazin USSR 639.25
1984

LIGHTWEIGHT (148.75 lbs.)
1976
Piotr Korol USSR 672.25
1980
Yanko Russev Bulgaria 755
1984

MIDDLEWEIGHT (165 lbs.)
1976
Yordan Mitkov Bulgaria 738.5
1980
Asen Zlatev Bulgaria 793.5
1984

LIGHT-HEAVYWEIGHT (181.5 lbs.)
1976
Valeri Shary USSR 804.5
1980
Yurik Vardanyan USSR 881.75
1984

MIDDLE-HEAVYWEIGHT (198.25 lbs.)
1976
David Rigert USSR 843.25
1980
Peter Baczako USSR 832
1984

MIDDLE-HEAVYWEIGHT (220.25 lbs.)
1976
Event not held
1980
Ota Zaremba Czechoslovakia 870.75
1984

HEAVYWEIGHT (242.5 lbs.)
1976
Yuri Zaitzev USSR 848.75
1980
Leonid Taranenko USSR 931.25
1984

SUPER-HEAVYWEIGHT (Over 242.5 lbs.)
1976
Vassili Alexeyev USSR 970
1980
Sultan Rakhmanov USSR 970
1984

WRESTLING
FREESTYLE
LIGHT FLYWEIGHT (106 lbs.)
1976
Hassan Issaev Bulgaria
1980
Claudio Pollio Italy
1984

FLYWEIGHT (114 lbs.)
1976
Yuji Takada Japan
1980
Anatoli Beloglazov USSR
1984

BANTAMWEIGHT (125 lbs.)
1976
Vladimir Umin USSR
1980
Sergei Beloglazov USSR
1984

FEATHERWEIGHT (136 lbs.)
1976
Jung-Mo Yang South Korea
1980
Magomedgasan
    Abushev USSR
1984

LIGHTWEIGHT (149 lbs.)
1976
Pavel Pinigin USSR
1980
Saipulla Absaidov USSR
1984

WELTERWEIGHT (163 lbs.)
1976
Jiichiro Date Japan
1980
Valentin Raitchev Bulgaria
1984

MIDDLEWEIGHT (180 lbs.)
1976
John Peterson United States
1980
Ismail Abilov Bulgaria
1984

LIGHT-HEAVYWEIGHT (198 lbs.)
1976
Levan Tediashvili USSR
1980
Sanasar Oganesyan USSR
1984

HEAVYWEIGHT (220 lbs.)
1976
Ivan Yarygin USSR
1980
Ilya Mate USSR
1984

SUPER-HEAVYWEIGHT (Over 220 lbs.)
1976
Soslan Andiev USSR
1980
Soslan Andiev USSR
1984

GRECO-ROMAN
LIGHT-FLYWEIGHT (105 lbs.)
1976
Alexei Shumakov USSR
1980
Zaksylik Ushkempirov USSR
1984

FLYWEIGHT (114.5 lbs.)
1976
Vitaly Konstantinov   USSR
1980
Vakhtang Balgidze   USSR
1984

BANTAMWEIGHT (125.5 lbs.)
1976
Pertti Ukkola   Finland
1980
Shamil Serikov   USSR
1984

FEATHERWEIGHT (136.5 lbs.)
1976
Kazimierz Lipien   Poland
1980
Stilianos Migiakis   Greece
1984

LIGHTWEIGHT (150 lbs.)
1976
Suren Nalbandyan   USSR
1980
Stefan Rusu   Romania
1984

WELTERWEIGHT (163 lbs.)
1976
Anatoly Bykov   USSR
1980
Ferenc Kocsis   Hungary
1984

MIDDLEWEIGHT (181 lbs.)
1976
Momir Petkovic   Yugoslavia
1980
Gennady Korban   USSR
1984

LIGHT-HEAVYWEIGHT (198.5 lbs.)
1976
Valery Rezantsev   USSR
1980
Norbert Novenyi   Hungary
1984

HEAVYWEIGHT (220 lbs.)
1976
Nikolai Balboshin   USSR
1980
Gheorgi Raikov   Bulgaria
1984

SUPER-HEAVYWEIGHT (Over 220 lbs.)
1976
Aleksandr Kolchinski   USSR
1980
Aleksandr Kolchinski   USSR
1984

YACHTING
SOLING
1976
P. Jensen-
    V. Bandolowski-
    E. Hansen   Denmark
1980
P. Jensen-
    V. Bandolowski-
    E. Hansen   Denmark
1984

STAR
1976
Event not held
1980
Valentin Mankin-
    Aleksandr
    Muzychenko   USSR
1984

FLYING DUTCHMAN
1976
Jorg Diesch-
    Eckart Diesch   West Germany
1980
Alejandro Abascal-
    Miguel Noguer   Spain
1984

470 CLASS
1976
Frank Hubner-
    Harro Bode   West Germany
1980
Marcos Soares-
    Eduardo Penido   Brazil
1984

FINN
1976
Jochen Schumann   East Germany
1980
Esko Rechardt   Finland
1984

TORNADO
1976
Reginald White-
    John Osborn   Britain
1980
Alexandre Welter-
    Lars Bjorkstrom   Brazil
1984

BOARDSAILING
1976
Event not held
1980
Event not held
1984

WORLD AND OLYMPIC RECORDS

TRACK AND FIELD

MEN
WORLD

Event	Mark	Name	Country	Year
100	9.93	Calvin Smith	United States	1983
200	21.72	Pietro Mennea	Italy	1979
400	43.86	Lee Evans	United States	1968
800	1:41.73	Sebastian Coe	Britain	1981
1,500	3:30.77	Steve Ovett	Britain	1983
5,000	13:00.41	Dave Moorcroft	Britain	1982
10,000	27:22.4	Henry Rono	Kenya	1978
110 Hurdles	12.93	Ronaldo Nehemiah	United States	1981
400 Hurdles	47.02	Edwin Moses	United States	1983
Steeplechase	8:05.4	Henry Rono	Kenya	1978
Marathon	2:08:12	Alberto Salazar	United States	1981
20-Km. Walk	1:20:06	Daniel Bautista	Mexico	1979
(road)	1:18:49	Daniel Bautista	Mexico	1979
50-Km. Walk	3:41:39	Raul Gonzales	Mexico	1979
(road)	3:37:36	Yevgeniy Ivchenko	USSR	1980
	3:37:36	Boris Yakovlyev	USSR	1980
4x100 Relay	37.86		United States	1983
4x400 Relay	2:56.16		United States	1968
High Jump	7-9¾	Zhu Jianhua	China	1983
Pole Vault	19-1½	Thierry Vigneron	France	1983
Long Jump	29-2½	Bob Beamon	United States	1968
Triple Jump	58-8½	Joao de Oliveira	Brazil	1975
Shot Put	72-10¾	Udo Beyer	East Germany	1983
Discus	235-9	Yuri Dumchev	USSR	1983
Hammer	276-0	Sergey Litvinov	USSR	1983
Javelin	327-2	Tom Petranoff	United States	1983
Decathlon	8779	Jurgen Hingsen	West Germany	1983

OLYMPIC

Event	Mark	Name	Country	Year
100	9.95	James Hines	United States	1968
200	19.83	Tommie Smith	United States	1968
400	43.86	Lee Evans	United States	1968
800	1:43.50	Alberto Juantorena	Cuba	1976
1,500	3:34.91	Kip Keino	Kenya	1968
5,000	13:20.34	Brendan Foster	Britain	1976
10,000	27:38.35	Lasse Viren	Finland	1972
110 Hurdles	13.24	Rod Milburn	United States	1972
400 Hurdles	47.64	Edwin Moses	United States	1976
Steeplechase	8:08.02	Anders Garderud	Sweden	1976
Marathon	2:09:55	Waldemar Cierpinski	East Germany	1976
20-Km. Walk	1:23:36	Maurizio Damilano	Italy	1980
50-Km. Walk	3:49:24	Hartwig Gauder	East Germany	1980
4x100 Relay	38.19		United States	1968
	38.19		United States	1972
4x400 Relay	2:56.16		United States	1968
High Jump	7-9	Gerd Wessig	East Germany	1980
Pole Vault	18-11½	Waldimir Kozakiewicz	Poland	1980
Long Jump	29-2½	Bob Beamon	United States	1968
Triple Jump	57-0¾	Viktor Saneyev	USSR	1968
Shot Put	70-0½	Vladimir Kiselyov	USSR	1980
Discus	221-5	Mac Wilkins	United States	1976
Hammer	268-4	Yuri Sedykh	USSR	1980
Javelin	310-4	Miklos Nemeth	Hungary	1976
Decathlon	8,618	Bruce Jenner	United States	1976

WOMEN
WORLD

Event	Mark	Name	Country	Year
100	10.79	Evelyn Ashford	United States	1983
200	21.71	Marita Koch	East Germany	1979
400	47.99	Jarmila Kratochvilova	Czechoslovakia	1983
800	1:53.28	Jarmila Kratochvilova	Czechoslovakia	1983
1,500	3:52.47	Tatyana Kazankina	USSR	1980
3,000	8:26.78	Svyetlana Ulmasova	USSR	1982
100 Hurdles	12.36	Grazyna Rabsztyn	Poland	1980
400 Hurdles	54.02	Anna Ambraziene	USSR	1983
Marathon	2:22:43	Joan Benoit	United States	1983
4x100 Relay	41.53		East Germany	1983
4x400 Relay	3:19.04		East Germany	1983
High Jump	6-8¼	Tamara Bykova	USSR	1983
Long Jump	24-4½	Anisoara Cusmir	Romania	1983
Shot Put	73-8	Ilona Slupianek	Czechoslovakia	1980
Discus	240-4	Galina Savinkova	USSR	1983
Javelin	245-3	Tiina Lillak	Finland	1983
Heptathlon	6,836	Ramona Neubert	East Germany	1983

OLYMPIC

Event	Mark	Name	Country	Year
100	11.01	Annegret Richter	West Germany	1976
200	22.03	Barbel Wockel	East Germany	1980
400	48.88	Marita Koch	East Germany	1980
800	1:53.43	Nadezhda Olizarenko	USSR	1980
1,500	3:56.6	Tatyana Kazankina	USSR	1980
3,000	Not previously held			
Marathon	Not previously held			
100 Hurdles	12.56	Vera Komisova	USSR	1980
400 Hurdles	Not previously held			
4x100 Relay	41.60		East Germany	1980
4x400 Relay	3:19.23		East Germany	1976
High Jump	6-5½	Sara Simeoni	Italy	1980
Long Jump	23-2	Tatiana Kolpakova	USSR	1980
Shot Put	73-6¼	Ilona Slupianek	East Germany	1980
Discus	229-6	Evelin Jahl	East Germany	1980
Javelin	224-5	Maria Colon	Cuba	1980
Heptathlon	Not previously held			

SWIMMING

MEN
WORLD

Event	Time	Name	Country	Year
100 Freestyle	49.36	Ambrose Gaines	United States	1981
200 Freestyle	1:47.87	Michael Gross	West Germany	1983
400 Freestyle	3:48.32	Vladimir Salnikov	USSR	1983
1,500 Freestyle	14:54.76	Vladimir Salnikov	USSR	1983
100 Backstroke	55.19	Rick Carey	United States	1983
200 Backstroke	1:58.93	Rick Carey	United States	1983
100 Breaststroke	1:02.28	Steve Lundquist	United States	1983
200 Breaststroke	2:14.77	Victor Davis	Canada	1982
100 Butterfly	53.44	Matt Gribble	United States	1983
200 Butterfly	1:57.05	Michael Gross	West Germany	1983
200 Ind. Medley	2:02.25	Alex Baumann	Canada	1982
400 Ind. Medley	4:19.78	Ricardo Prado	Brazil	1982
4x100 Medley Relay	3:40.42		United States	1983
4x100 Freestyle Relay	3:19.26		United States	1982
4x200 Freestyle Relay	7:20.40		United States	1983

OLYMPIC

Event	Time	Name	Country	Year
100 Freestyle	49.99	Jim Montgomery	United States	1976
200 Freestyle	1:49.81	Sergey Kopliakov	USSR	1980
400 Freestyle	3:51.31	Vladimir Salnikov	USSR	1980
1,500 Freestyle	14:58.27	Vladimir Salnikov	USSR	1980
100 Backstroke	55.49	John Nabor	United States	1976
200 Backstroke	1:59.19	John Nabor	United States	1976
100 Breaststroke	1:03.11	John Hencken	United States	1976
200 Breaststroke	2:15.11	David Wilkie	Britain	1976
100 Butterfly	54.27	Mark Spitz	United States	1972
200 Butterfly	1:59.23	Michael Bruner	United States	1976
200 Ind. Medley	2:07.17	Gunnar Larsson	Sweden	1972
400 Ind. Medley	4:22.89	Aleksandr Sidorenko	USSR	1980
4x100 Medley Relay	3:42.22		United States	1976

4x100 Free-style Relay	3:26.42		United States	1976
4x200 Free-style Relay	7:23.22		United States	1976

WOMEN
WORLD
100 Freestyle	54.79	Barbara Krause	East Germany	1980
200 Freestyle	1:58.23	Cynthia Woodhead	United States	1979
400 Freestyle	4:06.28	Tracey Wickham	Australia	1978
800 Freestyle	8:24.62	Tracey Wickham	Australia	1978
100 Back-stroke	1:00.86	Rica Reinisch	East Germany	1980
200 Back-stroke	2:09.91	Cornelia Sirch	East Germany	1982
100 Breast-stroke	1:08.51	Ute Geweniger	East Germany	1983
200 Breast-stroke	2:28.36	Julia Bogdanova	East Germany	1979
100 Butterfly	57.93	Mary T. Meagher	United States	1981
200 Butterfly	2:05.96	Mary T. Meagher	United States	1981
200 Ind. Medley	2:11.73	Ute Geweniger	East Germany	1981
400 Ind. Medley	4:36.10	Petra Schneider	East Germany	1982
4x100 Medley Relay	4:05.79		East Germany	1983
4x100 Free-style Relay	3:42.71		East Germany	1980

OLYMPIC
100 Freestyle	54.79	Barbara Krause	East Germany	1980
200 Freestyle	1:58.33	Barbara Krause	East Germany	1980
400 Freestyle	4:08.76	Ines Diers	East Germany	1980
800 Freestyle	8:29.90	Michelle Ford	Australia	1980
100 Back-stroke	1:00.86	Rica Reinisch	East Germany	1980
200 Back-stroke	2:11.77	Rica Reinisch	East Germany	1980
100 Breast-stroke	1:10.11	Ute Geweniger	East Germany	1980
200 Breast-stroke	2:29.54	Lina Kachushite	USSR	1980
100 Butterfly	1:00.13	Cornelia Ender	East Germany	1976
200 Butterfly	2:10.44	Ines Geissler	East Germany	1976
200 Ind. Medley	2:23.07	Shane Gould	Australia	1972
400 Ind. Medley	4:36.29	Petra Schneider	East Germany	1980
4x100 Medley Relay	4:06.67		East Germany	1980
4x100 Free-style Relay	3:42.71		East Germany	1980

WEIGHTLIFTING
WORLD
FLYWEIGHT (114.61 lbs)

Neno Terzynski	Bulgaria	573 lbs.	1983

BANTAMWEIGHT (123 lbs.)

Niam Suleimanov	Bulgaria	649 lbs.	1983

FEATHERWEIGHT (132 lbs.)

Yuri Sarkisyan	USSR	688 lbs.	1983

LIGHTWEIGHT (148.75 lbs.)

Joachim Kunz	East Germany	760 lbs.	1981

MIDDLEWEIGHT (165 lbs.)

Aleksandr Varbanov	Bulgaria	815 lbs.	1983

LIGHT-HEAVYWEIGHT (181.5 lbs.)

Yurik Vardanyan	USSR	881.75 lbs.	1980

MIDDLE-HEAVYWEIGHT (198.25 lbs.)

Blagoi Blagoev	Bulgaria	925 lbs.	1983

MIDDLE-HEAVYWEIGHT (220.25 lbs.)

Yuri Zakharevich	USSR	970 lbs.	1983

HEAVYWEIGHT (242.5 lbs.)

Vyacheslav Klokov	USSR	970 lbs.	1983

SUPER-HEAVYWEIGHT (Over 242.5 lbs.)

Aleksandr Gunyushev	USSR	1,019 lbs.	1983

OLYMPIC
FLYWEIGHT (114.61 lbs.)

Kanykek Osmanoliev	USSR	540 lbs.	1980
Ho-Bong Choi	North Korea	540 lbs.	1980
Han-Gyong Si	North Korea	540 lbs.	1980
Bela Olah	Hungary	540 lbs.	1980

BANTAMWEIGHT (123 lbs.)

Daniel Nunez	Cuba	606.25 lbs.	1980

FEATHERWEIGHT (132 lbs.)

Viktor Mazin	USSR	639.25 lbs.	1980

LIGHTWEIGHT (148.75 lbs.)

Yanko Russev	Bulgaria	755 lbs.	1980

MIDDLEWEIGHT (165 lbs.)

Asen Zlatev	Bulgaria	793.5 lbs.	1980

LIGHT-HEAVYWEIGHT (181.5 lbs.)

Yurik Vardanyan	USSR	881.75 lbs.	1980

MIDDLE-HEAVYWEIGHT (191.75 lbs.)

David Rigert	USSR	843.25 lbs.	1976

MIDDLE-HEAVYWEIGHT (220.25 lbs.)

Ota Zaremba	Czechoslo-vakia	870.75 lbs.	1980

HEAVYWEIGHT (242.5 lbs.)

Leonid Taranenko	USSR	931.25 lbs.	1980

SUPER-HEAVYWEIGHT (Over 242.5 lbs.)

Vasiliy Alexeyev	USSR	970 lbs.	1976
Sultan Rakhmanov	USSR	970 lbs.	1980

GOLD MEDAL STANDINGS 1896-1980

United States	622	Greece	14
USSR	340	Austria	13
Britain	154		
Sweden	130	Argentina	13
France	129	India	8
East Germany (1956-80)	123	Mexico	7
Italy	121	Estonia	6
Hungary	111	Egypt	6
Finland	91	Ireland	5
Japan	73	Brazil	5
		Ethiopia	5
Germany (1896-1936)	70	Kenya	5
Australia	66	Jamaica	4
West Germany (1952-80)	50		
Czechoslovakia	42	Iran	4
Poland	38	Uruguay	2
Netherlands	36	Spain	2
Norway	36	Pakistan	2
Switzerland	36	North Korea	2
Belgium	32	Russia (1896-1912)	1
Romania	28	Peru	1
		Luxembourg	1
Bulgaria	27	Bahamas	1
Canada	26	Venezuela	1
Denmark	29		
Turkey	23	Tunisia	1
Cuba	23	Uganda	1
South Africa	16	Trinidad	1
Yugoslavia	16	South Korea	1
New Zealand	14	Zimbabwe	1

Acknowledgments

The Publisher wishes to thank the following persons, whose generous assistance has been invaluable in preparing this book: At the *Los Angeles Times* Syndicate: Willard Colston, Angela Rinaldi; at the *Los Angeles Times*: John Foley, George Kiseda, Ken Reich, Joan Stern, and especially Jim Wilson, Cindy Hively (Photo Department).